EXERCISES IN TEACHING COMMUNICATION

Stewart Marshall and Noel Williams

Kogan
Page

313510

First published in Great Britain in 1986 by
Kogan Page Ltd, 120 Pentonville Road, London N1 9JN

British Library Cataloguing in Publication Data
Marshall, Stewart
    Exercises in teaching communication.
    1. Communication
    I. Title   II. Williams, Noel
    302.2   P90

    ISBN 1-85091-055-3

Printed in Great Britain by
Billing and Sons Ltd, Worcester

Contents

Acknowledgements

We would like to thank all the staff and students at Sheffield City Polytechnic who produced ideas for, participated in, and evaluated the exercises in this book.

Acknowledgements

Introduction

This is a handbook and materials source for teachers of communication. It provides a collection of exercises and source materials on most aspects of communication, oriented particularly towards communication for science, engineering and business students in further and higher education. Teachers of communication in schools will also find most of the exercises suitable for their needs. We have designed them with both schools and colleges in mind. Many can be used at any level with no adaptation. Where an exercise is more appropriate to one level rather than another we have included in the list of variations which accompanies each exercise suggestions for suitable adaptation. Teachers will find both modular packages on particular areas of communication and a number of course designs using selections from those modules. The exercises concentrate on the teaching of communication skills rather than theory; consequently they are primarily experiential and practical. The aim is to build in communication theory only as support for or development from relevant communication skills. However, there is provision for a more theoretical course within the modules to allow as varied an approach as is desired.

The book is intended primarily for teachers of communication, particularly teachers of communication skills for science, engineering and business students. This includes teachers with little experience in communication skills training who wish to incorporate such material within their discipline; teachers who wish to broaden the base of a technical course; and teachers of English for technical courses; as well as teachers within pure communication courses.

The first section of the book describes its rationale, its experiential, skills-based philosophy and the strategy by which it is organized. The next section consists of 38 exercises in communication. These are grouped according to general subject matter (written presentation, group organization, etc).

In the final section, there are a number of outlines of courses using these exercises, designed for particular types of syllabuses, particular objectives or particular strategies of teaching.

Section A:
Communication

What exactly do we mean when we say that we are 'teaching communication'?

In this section we give a brief outline of the rationale of teaching communication. We also consider the various ways in which such teaching has been incorporated in science, engineering and business education. Finally, we outline the philosophy of the book — its experiential and skills-based approach to teaching communication.

The call for more communication and related skills

For many years there has been some concern about the effectiveness of training students for their future careers. This concern is manifest in schools through the desire to produce students with the skills in presentation and communication necessary for obtaining employment or a satisfactory place in higher education. Similarly, in further and higher education themselves, the concern is not particularly with deficiencies in subject knowledge. Instead, the concern is expressed in terms of such factors as 'poor personal motivation and little professional commitment; lack of flexibility, breadth of vision and creativity in problem solving; need of close supervision; and deficiencies in interpersonal and communicative skills' (CBI, 1976). For example, the Finniston Report (1980) identified most of these qualities and skills as being those required by British employers but found lacking in engineering graduates.

Of course, the problem is not unique to Britain — the same concerns are expressed, for example, in Belgium (Van den Berghe, 1983) and the USA (Albright and Albright, 1981).

Clearly, vocational courses should include the development of these non-cognitive attitudes and skills among their objectives. In Britain, at diploma and certificate level, the Business and Technician Education Council (BTEC) affirmed this, insisting on the inclusion of such objectives in their courses. Consequently, we find that science, engineering and business courses often include the teaching of communication and related skills as part of the curriculum. However, what is taught varies considerably (Hills *et al.*, 1979).

In schools we find an increasing move to teach students those skills which will allow them to study, work and communicate more effectively, whatever the discipline they intend to pursue. One can sometimes identify, however, a failure to appreciate the nature or range of skills that may be needed, and most students may receive significant tuition only in discipline-based skills.

What is meant by 'communication skills'?

In the various courses one can identify four general areas that are seen as important:

1. *Receiver skills:* including study skills, information retrieval and note-taking;
2. *Presentation skills:* including oral, written and visual presentation skills;
3. *Skills in communicating person to person:* including interviewing and being interviewed;
4. *Skills in working in groups:* including participating in and leading groups and running meetings.

The exercises in this book can be seen to fall into these categories.

How can we include communication skills in the course?

There would seem to be three possible ways of including the teaching of communication skills in a course:

1. By establishing a discrete syllabus for this teaching;
2. By including the teaching in one or two other syllabuses; or
3. By teaching communication skills throughout the whole course.

Surveys of communication skills teaching (Hills *et al.*, 1979; Railton, 1984) show that examples of each method can readily be found in science, engineering and business education. The decision as to which method is most appropriate or which one is likely to succeed, is a complicated one. Among other things, it would seem to be a function of the expertise and personality of the tutor; the age, experience and motivation of the students; and the time available.

In many institutions, the planning of science and engineering courses for the Technician Education Council in the mid-1970s created discrete 'communication studies' syllabuses. At the same time, such syllabuses also appeared in many science and engineering degree courses. Within schools, it has also been the case that communication skills, where taught, have been taught as discrete syllabuses, perhaps replacing the older General Studies, and are thus frequently perceived by pupils as peripheral to the discipline-based studies which form the focus of their education. Unfortunately, but perhaps not surprisingly, some of these discrete courses in communication studies do not seem to have met with much success.

A common criticism of such courses is that students do not see them as relevant to their main studies. It has been argued in further and higher education that part of this problem is timing — many communication studies courses are designed to run in the first year of the student's study. Wilcox (1980) argues that courses in communication are more effective near the end of programmes when students are more mature, receptive and able to see the need for communication skills. In schools this argument would seem invalid as, where communication is taught, it usually occurs towards the end of a student's schooling. However, if we are to improve these skills, surely we need to help the students as early as possible?

The problem of 'relevance' is a serious one for discrete courses in communication studies. Because of their 'discrete' nature, there is an inherent danger that such courses can easily become (or be seen as) detached from and peripheral to the main educational activities. The Business and Technician Education Council (BTEC) emphasizes the need to situate the study of communication in the real world and not to detach it from the circumstances in which it operates. Thus, one finds that many BTEC courses use the second and third approaches listed above.

In engineering education one also finds examples of the second and third approaches. Where communication skills are taught in the context of an engineering syllabus, ie in a 'combined' course such as 'Industrial and Communication Studies', students more readily perceive the relevance. Such combined courses seem to be successful, especially where they are 'team-taught' by communication and engineering specialists (Blanchard and Marshall, 1980; Railton, 1984).

Gray (1979) argues that a 'between-the-lines' approach to teaching communication skills is the most appropriate for engineers. He proposes that the skills should be taught throughout the whole engineering course, as part of the normal engineering exercise. Such an approach has much to recommend it. Unlike the discrete course, it does not appear to add unwanted hours to the student's timetable. Also, because of the integration, the communication skills training is perceived as relevant. However, there are some problems with this method — mostly associated with ensuring that the staff and time are committed to a unified and informed approach to developing the skills.

Other problems arise in assessment. For example, in a school course heavily oriented towards a final examination, neither tutor nor student may see much sense in devoting time to skills which are not directly being assessed in that exam. Here communication skills become little more than the skills needed to pass a given type of examination.

How are we to teach communication skills?

Part of the problem experienced by teachers of discrete courses in communication studies may well be the teaching method — the attempt to teach communication starting from a theoretical perspective. Lectures may enable engineering students to answer exam questions about the process of communication, but are unlikely to improve their communicative ability. Similarly, a lecture on the psychology of motivation may be of theoretical interest to a few business students, but will do little to improve their personal motivation. To many students such lectures are seen as unwelcome additions to already full timetables.

Wilcox (1980) comments on the need to adjust both the teaching method and the content in a communication course to the particular audience. This is, of course, the first principle of course design. So what exactly does it entail?

Clearly, practice is required to improve skills. But the practical work must be made relevant, otherwise the students lack the interest and motivation required to achieve the desired objectives. The practical work must also be realistic, otherwise students will fail to transfer any learning that has taken place. Wherever possible, we would make a plea that practical work should be undertaken in groups. In addition to the added realism that this brings to problem solving, there are many other gains (as we discuss below).

There is a role for theory here too, for without some theory the students will be unlikely to generalize or apply their learning to other situations. But, for the majority of science, engineering and business courses, the theory should be introduced in order to support this 'generalization' process, and not taught as an end in itself.

Within schools it is arguable that a general studies approach has more chance of success, at least at the level of raising students' awareness. If such a course seeks to integrate communication skills with a study of wider social and cultural aspects of communication, the inherent attraction of work on the media, youth culture or non-verbal communication, for example, may sufficiently motivate a student to pursue more mundane aspects of communication study. Conversely, one may argue that the gains within such a discrete school syllabus in communication are only truly of value if the skills learned can successfully be carried across to other subjects, and this seldom seems to be the case.

Experiential/activity-based teaching

A survey of the literature shows that games and simulations are often claimed to have considerable success in overcoming the problem of student interest, attitude and motivation (Garvey, 1971; Ellington *et al.*, 1981; Marshall, 1982).

First, some definitions. A *simulation* is a dynamic representation of the central features of a real situation (Gibbs, 1974; Bloomer, 1973; Percival and Ellington, 1980). By *game* we mean an activity in which decision makers, operating within rules, compete to achieve their objectives (Abt, 1968; Gibbs, 1974; Bloomer, 1973). Clearly, games and simulations overlap to a great extent. Although there are games which are not simulations, those which are of interest for the teaching of communication skills normally involve simulation. By *experiential exercise* we mean an activity by means of which the student is able to experience, in a safe environment, some selected aspect of reality. Such exercises will often involve simulation, but will not always be games.

Thus, what happens in the activity-based teaching which we are considering is that:

1. Students are presented with problems which are representative of those in their future adult and professional world;

2. Either as themselves or in some adopted role they make decisions and act in response to the problem;
3. They may experience simulated consequences as a result of their decisions and performance;
4. They reflect upon their experiences and the results of their actions.

We would argue that this form of teaching (involving games, simulations and similar forms of experiential exercises) is most appropriate both for the kind of material to be taught and the kind of student being given that material.

Wherever possible, the activities should involve group work. There are several advantages to this. Perhaps the most important are that it facilitates peer group learning and support. Both these factors are important in any class, but are particularly so in the large classes that are commonly experienced now. At the start of a course, a group exercise can also serve the valuable function of introducing students to one another. It also introduces them to the idea of working together in groups — usually a skill area that we wish to cover anyway.

In conclusion then, in order to develop the desired attitudes and skills, major changes in teaching methods are required — changes not only in the teaching of communication, but also in the teaching of the other subjects. Can anyone reasonably expect the one or two hours per week spent on communication studies to achieve much, especially when submerged by many hours of traditional teaching?

Commenting on communication skills in engineering, Gray (1981) suggests that there is no need for a discrete course in communication at all. We would agree, providing teaching methods change elsewhere in the course. Ideally, simulation, games and other experiential exercises should be used to teach (or reinforce) some of the main science, engineering or business content of courses. This would then provide appropriate situations to be used for the development of the desired non-cognitive skills and attitudes. This integration of the cognitive and non-cognitive aspects would ensure that students correctly perceive the importance of both in their education.

The Exercises

This section consists of 38 exercises arranged under topic headings. The orientation of the exercises is towards the science, engineering and business student, though many of them have wider applications.

A list of the topics and exercises is given here to facilitate quick reference.

List of topics and exercises

Topic 1: Study skills

Topic 2: Written presentation

Topic 3: Oral presentation

3.5   A group talk on alternative energy
3.6   Visual aids
3.7   Developing a point

Topic 4: Interpersonal communication

4.1   Introduction to interpersonal communication
4.2   Questioning skills
4.3   Introduction to non-verbal communication

Topic 5: Interviewing

5.1   Information-gathering interviews
5.2   Assessment interviews
5.3   The structure of selection interviews
5.4   Interviewer skills in selection interviews
5.5   Thinking about being interviewed
5.6   Interviewee skills in selection interviews
5.7   Self-motivation

Topic 6: Group communication

6.1   Introduction to group work
6.2   Group organization
6.3   Decision making
6.4   Group decision making

Topic 7: Theory of communication

7.1   Information processing
7.2   Language, grammar and algorithms
7.3   Redundancy
7.4   The functions of language

The format of the exercises

Each of the exercises in this section is described using the following format:

Exercise number

Title of the exercise

Aims:
What the exercise is designed to do.

Equipment and materials required:
List of student materials (information sheets, worksheets, etc) and number required, plus any other equipment and materials needed.

Time required:
The usual time required to run the exercise.

Procedure:
Brief description of how to run the exercise.

Information for the students:
Details for information sheets and briefing.

Supporting information for the tutor:
General information about the exercise, plus supporting material for lectures or other tutor input.

Other notes:
Summary of the main points that the students need to know (if appropriate).

Supporting bibliography and references:
List of published items useful for the tutor and/or the students.

Variations:
Ways in which the exercise could be varied.

Related exercises: (in other topics).

Topic 1: Study skills

Exercise 1.1

Library search: annotating a reading list

Aims:

1. To introduce students to the library;
2. To encourage organized literature searching and note-taking;
3. To encourage self-evaluation of information-gathering techniques.

Equipment and materials required:
Briefing sheet for each class member.

Time required: (minimum 60 minutes)
You will need five minutes to explain the exercise, which will then take the students about one hour to complete.

Procedure:
Give each member of the class a briefing sheet (see 'Information for the students' below). Explain the background to the task and give the instructions for completing it. You may find it necessary to give an example of the type of flow chart required for instruction (1), and also the referencing convention to be used for instruction (3). The students are then told to complete the exercise in the library, and to hand in their results for marking.

Information for the students:
The briefing for the library search:

LIBRARY SEARCH ON ALTERNATIVE ENERGY

A. Background to the task: A proposal has been made for developing the Island of Elaskay, off the north-west coast of Scotland, as an experimental site for the production of electricity by means of alternative energy. You have been asked, by the Council of Elaskay, to prepare a short list of key texts on *one* source of alternative energy, and to describe briefly the content of each text.

B. Instructions: Complete the following:
1. Draw a flow chart mapping your actual information search in the library.
2. Produce a list of all the materials (books, articles, chapters) you look at, with a few words describing each item.
3. From your list, select *four* items which the Council of Elaskay might find useful. For *each* of these items, write about 50 words describing the content. (Remember to use the appropriate referencing conventions.)

Supporting information for the tutor:
This exercise needs very little introduction from the tutor, though it may need some support by the library staff. The exercise works well if the briefing sheet is given immediately prior to an introductory tour around the library, and then completed immediately after.

Ideally, the exercise should form the initial stage of a longer exercise (eg writing a report, or giving a short talk), as there is little incentive to conduct a literature search for its own sake. Thus, in introducing this exercise you may wish to set the scene for the subsequent exercise, or spend some time talking about alternative energy.

NOTE ON REFERENCING CONVENTIONS:
If your discipline, course or institution does not have its own clearly defined referencing conventions, it will be necessary to provide one for the students to use. Ensure that students recognize:

1. That they should follow the given convention *exactly* in the exercise and in all bibliographical work. (There is little point in having a convention if it is not adhered to.)
2. That they are using a convention, not an inviolable rule, and other different conventions exist. Where other bibliographies/references are quoted, the convention used in the quoted bibliography should be translated into that of the quoting bibliography.

The following is a widely used convention.

For books:
   Author, *Title*, publisher, (edition), place of publication, date of publication. Pages or chapter referred to if required.

For journals, magazines or papers:
   Author, 'title', *Journal*, volume, number, date, page number(s).
Alternatively use the referencing convention adopted in this book.

Supporting bibliography and references:
Fisher, Cassie W and Constantine, T (1977) *Student's Guide to Success.* Macmillan.

Variations:

1. Divide the class into small groups, and instruct each group to complete the exercise and hand in a communal answer sheet.

2. For the library search, rewrite the 'brief' using a topic from a 'main' subject on the course.

Related exercises: 3.5 and 6.1

■ Exercise 1.2

Library search: abstracts and summaries

Aims:

1. To introduce students to the library;
2. To encourage organized literature searching and note-taking;
3. To give the students practice in writing summaries;
4. To encourage the students to think about the nature and value of their own education;

21

5. To give the students practice in responding to published critical comment.

Equipment and materials required:
Briefing sheet for each class member.

Time required: (minimum 90 minutes)
You will need five minutes to explain the exercise, which will then take the students about 90 minutes to complete.

Procedure:
Give each member of the class a briefing sheet (see 'Information for the students' below). Explain the background to the task and give the instructions for completing it. You may need to give the students the referencing convention to be used for instruction (2). The students are then told to complete the exercise in the library and to hand in the results for marking.

Information for the students:
The briefing for the library search:

LIBRARY SEARCH ON YOUR PROFESSIONAL EDUCATION

A. Background to the task: You have been asked by a prospective employer to write a few paragraphs about your professional education and training at this institution. The employer wants you to explain why it is superior to others, and in what way it overcomes some of the criticisms (as found in government publications and reports by professional bodies) levelled at professional education and training.

B. Instructions: Complete the following:

1. Locate *five* items (chapters, articles, reports) in the library on education and training in your future profession.
2. Produce a list of these items, with a few words describing each item. (Remember to use the appropriate referencing conventions.)
3. From your list, select *one* item and write about 100 words summarizing the content.
4. Write about 300 words on your professional education and training at this institution. Try to relate what you write to the criticisms you discovered in your literature search (in particular, in the item selected for (3)).

Supporting information for the tutor:
Ideally, the exercise should form the initial stage of a longer exercise (eg writing a curriculum vitae, or simulating a selection interview). Thus, in introducing this exercise you may wish to set the scene for the subsequent exercise.

It is useful to introduce the exercise by reading some of the criticisms levelled against the education and training of the students' chosen profession. If this is then set in the context of the high rate of unemployment, students quickly realize that it is in their interests to ensure that they are receiving education and training which is creditable.

Supporting bibliography and references:
Fisher, Cassie W and Constantine, T (1977) *Student's Guide to Success.* Macmillan.

Variations:

1. *School variation (a)*
For schools it may not be appropriate to consider a vocational task of this kind because students may expect to pass directly into higher education. The tutor may adapt the task so that the information is required not by an employer but by a college or university. In particular, students might research comparable schools and courses, examination syllabuses from other examining boards and the academic history of former pupils. The exercise can also be used to sensitize students to aspects of their disciplines which are not part of the set curriculum by comparing the current curriculum with other possible curricula.

2. *School variation (b)*
The exercise may not be appropriate for schools because students would find it difficult to identify job-specific characteristics of their current education. In these circumstances the tutor may adapt the exercise so that the information is required for a local radio, TV or newspaper interview about the school. Here, students would be required to research their training and institution within the context of a wider debate about the nature of education in the chosen subject in the region. Students would be required to show what their course had to offer in order to enhance the image of the school, attract other pupils and attract local support and funding.

If the students respond best to dramatic scenarios this variant can be constructed within the fictional context of threatened closure of either the institution or the course, the proposed interview being part of a publicity drive to prevent such closure.

This variant can form part of an extended series of exercises which would also include writing the article and conducting the interview.

Related exercises: 2.4, 2.5 and 5.5.

■ **Exercise 1.3**

Taking notes

Aims:

1. To give students practice in taking notes;
2. To encourage students to evaluate their own note-taking techniques;
3. To make students familiar with one simple précis technique.

Equipment and materials required:
One copy of the test text for each student.

Time required: (minimum 15 minutes)
The exercise requires about two minutes for briefing and about 15 minutes to carry out.

Procedure:

Divide students into pairs and give each student a copy of the test paragraph. Students are to extract key information from the paragraph in five minutes, one using his/her own method and the other the method described below. Then each pair must compare notes and decide on which technique is most useful, using the questions provided. Where one technique proves more useful the pair should establish what its value is.

Information for the students:
Briefing for each pair:

> You have been given a short text from which you must each take notes extracting the key information. One of you must use your own method and the other must use the method described below. You will be given only five minutes to make your notes. When five minutes have elapsed compare notes and answer the questions at the end of this sheet.

> TEXT — AN INTRODUCTION TO LANGUAGE
> Language can be thought of as composed of a number of levels, whether we consider spoken or written language. At the lowest level is the raw material of language, the sounds that the vocal organs can make or the marks that writing instruments can make. These can be organized into meaningful signs, the phonemes of spoken language and the graphemes (including the alphabet) of written language. These basic symbols are limited in number. English, for example, has only 45 phonemes. These symbols can be combined together to make morphemes. Morphemes have their own shape and their own meaning being essentially the meaning-ful subunits of words. Linguists regard morphemes as the smallest units of meaning which can have independent existence, though

some morphemes can stand on their own. For example 'fish' has only one morpheme which is independent but 'fishy' has two, 'fish' and '-y' of which the second cannot stand on its own. Independent morphemes are called 'free' morphemes and dependent ones are called 'bound'.

The level above that of morphemes is that of words. Words can be linked together to form groups (or phrases) and groups linked together to form clauses. Clauses make sentences, the simplest sentence being a single clause. Sentences can be put together in different ways to form texts, such as to give verses, paragraphs or speeches. In addition, all of the levels above the phoneme can be said to have meaning.

NOTE-TAKING METHOD

1. Read through the paragraph and identify one main topic. Write this down as a main heading.
2. Create four or five subheadings to represent the main subtopics.
3. For each subheading write one further keyword or phrase for each sentence or conjoined clause that deals with that topic.
   (A conjoined clause is part of a sentence joined to the rest by a conjunction such as 'and' or 'but'.)

QUESTIONS TO ANSWER

Compare your two sets of notes and answer the following questions:

1. Does one method give a greater structure than the other? If so, why?
2. Does one method provide notes which are easier to remember than the other? If so, why?
3. Does one method yield more notes than the other? If so, are the extra words necessary? If they are deleted is anything lost? Why have those words been included?
4. Can one method be applied with greater speed?
5. What are the advantages and disadvantages of the two methods? Can they be usefully combined?

Supporting information for the tutor:

Students should be encouraged to think about their typical note-taking strategies. They should be asked to decide:

1. Why do they take notes?
2. In what circumstances do they not take notes?
3. What do they use notes for?
4. How do they organize their notes? Does that organization fit with the uses identified in (3)? Can the organization be improved?
5. Do they take enough, too many or too few notes?

Most students do not learn a conscious note-taking technique. By causing them to examine their own procedures, attention can be drawn to the lack of logic in most note-taking procedures. It is useful for students to evaluate their own techniques rather than for them to be harangued about the need for certain practices, as they are likely to find the switch to a totally new approach difficult and irritating. However, they may be susceptible to adapting existing methods and dropping poor practices if by their own reflection they come to realize their own defects.

Supporting bibliography and references:
Fisher, Cassie W and Constantine, T (1977) *Student's Guide to Success.* Macmillan.

Variations:
If more work on note-taking is required, ask each pair to produce their notes for the last class they attended. They should compare them and decide what differences there are and why they exist, by asking the questions listed on the handout.

■ **Exercise 1.4**

Examination technique

Aims:

1. To give students practice in answering exam questions;
2. To familiarize students with a simple scheme for generating and organizing information;
3. To encourage students to consider the nature of good and bad exam technique.

Equipment and materials required:
One copy of the 'Guide to Answering Exam Questions' sheet for each student. A copy of an exam question or past exam paper.

Time required: (minimum 30 minutes)
The exercise requires only two minutes' briefing, and about 15 minutes for each question the students are expected to answer.

Procedure:
Brief the class and issue the guide sheets and exam questions. Tell the class the number of questions to be attempted and

warn them that only 15 minutes will be allowed for each answer. Students should then answer the questions. There is no need for a plenary session as undertaking the exercise itself should give students sufficient ideas on their own technique and some practice in applying the approach to typical exam questions.

Information for the students:

Briefing:

> You have been given a set of exam questions and a sheet describing a technique used for answering questions. Apply the technique to each question using no more than 15 minutes for each answer. Do not attempt to construct complete answers but ensure that they contain all the components demanded by the technique. When you have completed all the questions ask yourself:
>
> 1. Does the resulting answer include everything you would normally want to include?
> 2. Is the technique helpful?
> 3. Does the technique produce fuller answers than you would normally produce?
> 4. Is the technique an efficient use of time in an exam room?
>
> From your answers to these questions you should be able to decide whether this approach is one you will profit from in a real exam and, if not, what aspects of your technique are efficient or inefficient.

'A GUIDE TO ANSWERING EXAM QUESTIONS'

1. Read the question carefully.
2. Write down the three main words in the question.
3. Create a 'brain pattern' (see exercise 3.2) around these three words. Do not finish the pattern until you have at least 20 items in your pattern, but write items down as quickly as possible.
4. Now examine the question in detail. Write down one or more objections to it and integrate them in your brain pattern.
5. Break the question down into two or more sections. Write down a point in support of or in opposition to each part. Incorporate these in your brain pattern.
6. Examine the question for any ambiguity or hidden assumptions. If you find any, incorporate them in the brain pattern.
7. Write down two pieces of specific evidence, such as quotations, statistics or key facts that are, in your opinion, central to the question.

8. You now have everything you should need to write an adequate to good answer to your question. Your introduction should be formed around one of the two key pieces of evidence you wrote down and your conclusion around the other one.

9. The remainder of your answer will be constructed from the rest of the brain pattern. Those items in the pattern with many branches coming out of them are major topics and should form the basis of paragraphs or pages in your argument. Items connected to these main topics are subsections of the main paragraphs/pages which may have distinct subheadings. Items with only one branch are totally dependent on other ideas and, therefore, are unlikely to be more than single sentences or clauses.

10. Using this scheme order the items in your brain pattern as a list of headings and subheadings (and possible sub-subheadings).

11. You now have a complete plan of your answer containing introduction, conclusion, organized sections and at least 20 key points. All you have to do is turn the sectioned list of headings into a series of paragraphs and sentences.

Supporting information for the tutor:
Students need prior knowledge of and practice in creating brain patterns (see exercise 3.2). Tutors should make clear that the approach is not suitable for certain types of examinations, such as mathematical and scientific exams, being mainly valuable for discursive questions. Some students who already have clearly defined revision and exam techniques may find that an approach like this interferes with their normal practices and may therefore find the technique harmful rather than useful. Where students do object to such an approach, discuss the reasons underlying possible difficulties. The tutor should also make clear that familiarity with an approach like this will affect its usefulness, especially the time taken to produce an answer. Consequently it is in the student's interest to practise the technique.

Supporting bibliography and references:
Buzan, T (1982) *Using Your Head.* BBC Publications.
Deverell, C S (1973) *Successful Communication.* G Bell & Sons.
Fisher, Cassie W and Constantine, T (1977) *Student's Guide to Success.* Macmillan.

Variations:

1. If desired, a brief revision lecture and/or talk on exam technique can preface the exercise. Alternatively, this can follow the exercise, if the tutor feels that students' commentaries on their performance and the adequacy of the approach will reinforce learning or generate useful discussion. However, because the approach is quite rigorous, debate is likely to be couched purely in terms of like and dislike.

2. The exams can be marked and feedback given to students on likely performance, assuming that questions have been worked fully into complete answers.

3. An experiment can be performed with one half of the class answering a 40-minute exam question using the above method and the other half using their traditional approach. The division should be arbitrary. Answers should be marked and the mean for each group used as a measure of the efficacy of the technique. For a more rapid estimate of the net performance of each group, each student can count the length of his/her answer in words, or the tutor can roughly estimate the number of useful points made in each answer.

Topic 2: Written presentation

■ Exercise 2.1

Effective presentation

Aims:

1. To encourage students to think about some of the problems in presenting information effectively;
2. To enable students to share ideas about effective presentation;
3. To encourage students to use sectioning, ordering, numbering, labelling, upper case and spacing for more effective presentation.

Equipment and materials required:
Sufficient copies of the *Instruction Manual* extract for all the class. Large sheets of paper (eg from a flipchart) and felt pens

sufficient for the number of students in the class divided by four.

Time required:
Approximately 35 minutes.

Procedure:
In stage 1 of this exercise, the class is divided into pairs and each pair asked to revise the written style of each sentence in the extract. After about 10 minutes, each pair should be joined with one other, and the resulting group of four asked to compare their revisions and produce an agreed set. Each group is then asked to write their set of instructions on a large sheet of paper, paying particular attention to the effectiveness of the presentation.

In the final stage of the exercise, selected groups present their instructions to the rest of the class for discussion. Allow a few minutes at the end to reinforce the main learning points.

Information for the students:
The students should be given the following brief:

STAGE 1 – In pairs (10 minutes):

(a) Convert each sentence in the extract into one which reads as 'real' English, and which also communicates its message effectively.

STAGE 2 – In fours (15 minutes):

(b) Share the revisions made in (a) and produce an agreed set.
(c) Organize this set of instructions in a format which communicates the information effectively and gives the correct emphasis.
(d) Write your set of instructions on the sheet of paper provided, paying particular attention to the presentation.
(e) Appoint someone to present your group's ideas to the rest of the class.

STAGE 3 – Whole class (10 minutes):

(f) Present ideas and discuss.

The *Instruction Manual* extract to be modified:

ATTENTION!

The present *Instruction Manual* contains the basic characteristics and essential operating principles of the XYZ camera and cannot be regarded as a handbook on photography. Due to ever-advancing development of the camera construction, there may occur minor differences between the text of the *Manual* and the construction of your camera. To make the operating of the photocell reliable and to increase its service, do not subject the photocell to the exposure of direct sunlight.

Screw out or screw in the lens only by the lens mounting ring. Do not rotate the shutter release button for any reason, while releasing the shutter, to avoid disengagement of the shutter cocking mechanism. Do not rotate the exposure time dial within the interval between 'B' and '500'. Always wind the shutter as far as it goes to avoid blank exposures. Before using the camera, make a thorough study of the handling rules and operating procedure of the camera.

Supporting information for the tutor:
One solution to this problem is as follows:

PLEASE NOTE

This manual applies only to the XYZ camera and is not designed as a general handbook on photography.

Before using your camera, make sure you are familiar with its features and how to operate them.

1. *Do not* expose the photocell to direct sunlight as this will affect its life and its reliability.
2. If you need to remove the lens, do so by rotating the lens mounting ring.
3. When you press and release the shutter release button, make sure *not* to turn it round. If you do, the mechanism might be disconnected.
4. *Do not* try to turn the exposure time dial between the marks 'B' and '500'.
5. Always wind the shutter round as far as it will go, in order to avoid either double or blank exposures.

NB. You may find minor differences between the camera you have bought and that described in this *Manual.* These are due to recent advances in design.

During the presentation and discussion of the sets of instructions, the following are some of the points that you should seek to elicit:

1. SECTIONING
To help the receiver to process the information, it is useful to divide it into small sections.

2. ORDERING
To help the receiver to comprehend the message, the sections should be ordered.

3. NUMBERING OR LABELLING
Presentation is more effective if the ordered sections are numbered and/or labelled.

4. SPACING

Use horizontal and vertical spacing to help show the section divisions and to emphasize the logic of the written presentation.

5. UPPER CASE AND UNDERLINING

Use upper case and underlining to distinguish headings and to emphasize important points.

6. OTHER MEDIA

Consider other media, eg visual aids or algorithms.

Supporting bibliography and references:
Stanton, N (1982) *What Do You Mean 'Communication'?*
An introduction to communication in business. Pan.
Stanton, N (1982) *The Business of Communicating.* Pan.

Variations:

1. Combine the pairs to form larger groups (six or eight students) in stage 2.
2. Use a suitable extract taken from scientific, engineering or business literature.

■ Exercise 2.2

An investigation report

Aims:

1. To introduce students to the benefits and problems of working in groups;
2. To guide the students through a 'systematic approach' to problem solving;
3. To reinforce the required content and organization of investigation reports.

Equipment and materials required:
Lecture materials and some means of giving the students the 'report briefing'.

Time required:
Minimum — two hours of class time spread over three or four consecutive sessions, plus two hours of student homework time.

Procedure:
The students are asked to work in groups of about three or four

to produce a report commenting on and making recommendations to improve the effectiveness of Freshers' Week at their
institution. They are asked to use a 'systematic approach to
report writing' (see 'Supporting information for the tutor').
One of the virtues of this approach is that it enables one to
divide the overall task into parts, so that it can be tackled over
several weeks. It is advisable to give the students some time in
each class session to enable them to plan, assign and co-ordinate
the group's work on the report.

In session 1, each group is asked to 'define the problem'.
Having done this, they then spend about 15 minutes 'brain-
storming' ideas about the possible content of the report. They
are also asked to prepare a short questionnaire (a useful 'homework' exercise), which members then use to gather information for the report. At least 20 minutes of one session should
be allowed for collating and interpreting the information
gathered, and assigning writing tasks. A similar amount of time
in the following session will be required for gathering the
various parts of the report together and writing the 'covering
parts', eg the contents page.

Information for the students:
The students should be given the following brief:

> As a small group of 'management consultants', you have been asked
> by the Students' Union to investigate and write a report on the
> effectiveness of Freshers' Week. (Write about 750 words per group
> member.)

Students will obviously need a lecture on the systematic approach to report writing, plus supporting information while
the report is being prepared.

Supporting information for the tutor:
There are several types of report which a student may use in
his or her working life. This exercise deals with 'investigation'
reports. These, as the name suggests, are used to report the
results of an investigation. Clearly the students need to know
about other types of report but, since the report-writing skills
required are the same for all types, it seems reasonable to
concentrate on one in order to develop these skills.

In tackling any communication problem, we advocate a
'systematic approach'. By this we mean that one should tackle
the problem in stages. All too often, students (and ourselves)
rush forward with a solution without having paused to consider
the problem. Thus, the first stage in writing an investigation

report should be problem definition. As can be seen in the lecture notes, answering the question 'What is the problem?' involves looking carefully at one's objectives, considering the readers, and ascertaining if there is an expected style and content.

The second stage of the systematic approach is the generation of ideas and collection of information. We recommend that students use something like Tony Buzan's 'brain patterns' (1982) to create ideas about what could be investigated and included in the report (see exercise 3.2).

The third stage is used to evaluate, interpret and select from the information collected in the previous stage. Again, one of the mistakes often made in problem solving is to evaluate ideas as soon as they are generated. This tends to stem the flow of ideas and can be particularly destructive in group problem solving. So, this third stage should be kept quite distinct from the previous one.

Having decided what information is to be presented, the next stage is to decide how to present it. We ask students to include the 10 major sections shown in the lecture notes. Clearly, other formats are possible, but the students do need a framework for their reports.

Having written the various sections, we then suggest that they should look carefully at how the report can be improved. In this final stage, there are really three main aspeccts to look at:

1. *Readability* — ie that short sentences are used wherever possible, and that the language is clear and simple;
2. *Organization* — that the material is divided into sections, subsections and paragraphs which are labelled (with headings) and logically ordered;
3. *Presentation* — that the text is neatly written (preferably typed), with effective use of space and visual aids.

Lecture notes on writing investigation reports:

1. WHAT IS THE PROBLEM?
   Objectives
   Audience
   Expected style and content

2. IDEAS/INFORMATION FOR ACHIEVING THE OBJECTIVES?
   Create ideas — brainstorm
   Draw pattern plans to organize ideas
   Collect information — questionnaire, discussion

3. WHAT INFORMATION IS TO BE PRESENTED?
   Identify topics — about five main ones
   Select material for the above
   Interpret data for main conclusions

4. HOW TO PRESENT IT?
   Title page — title, author, for whom, location, date
   Table of contents — main sections and page numbers
   Summary — brief synopsis of whole report
   Introduction — background, purpose, plan
   Method of investigation — how, when, where, with what
   Main study — results and discussion
   Conclusions — must follow from evidence
   Recommendations — a plan for action
   Bibliography — author, date, title, details
   Appendix — materials needed to make report complete

5. HOW CAN THE REPORT BE IMPROVED?
   Readability — short sentences, clear language
   Organization — sections logically ordered
   Presentation — neat, use visual aids and space

Supporting bibliography and references:
Buzan, T (1982) *Using Your Head*. BBC Publications.
Smithson, S (1984) *Business Communication Today*. ICSA
Publishing.

Variations:

1. The reports could be written by individual students.

2. The topic to be investigated could be how to improve lectures
   and seminars. Or, a topic could be selected in one of the
   other subjects in the course.

3. *School variation:*
   As schools generally do not have an equivalent to Freshers'
   Week another topic must be chosen. The characteristics of
   the topic should be:
   (a) that it has multiple aspects so a group is required to
       investigate it
   (b) that it is based around the school so students can use
       various immediate means of investigation, especially
       interview and questionnaire
   (c) that it is problem-based so the students can carry out

investigative research, producing novel conclusions and recommendations

Possible topics which fulfil these criteria include:
1. Improving the library
2. Changing methods of assessment
3. How to spend £1000 within the school to best educational advantage
4. Improving the public image of the school
5. Improving the school's Open Day
6. Investigating new subject areas that could be taught

There is, of course, no reason why such an investigation cannot be built around a real case study on some problem actually taking place within the school. This inevitably increases student motivation and may produce useful information. However, if attempted the tutor should ensure that the exercise will not conflict with the official project or cause potential friction between students and staff.

Related exercises: 3.4, 3.6 and 3.7.

■ Exercise 2.3

Memoranda and short reports

Aims:

1. To give students experience in memo and report writing under pressure;
2. To encourage the practice of brevity and precision in written communication;
3. To illustrate common problems that occur in normal business communication;
4. To encourage students to practise organization in the storage and retrieval of information.

Equipment and materials required:
One copy of each of the initial memoranda.

Time required: (minimum 60 minutes)
Approximately five minutes will be required for the briefing. Allow about 30 minutes for conducting the exercise and 15 minutes for plenary commentary. A short lecture will probably be needed before or after the exercise.

Procedure:

Divide the class into small groups of no less than three members. Outline the scenario, then give each group a copy of one of the initial memoranda. Each group should have a different memo. Each group is then to behave according to the fiction of the scenario and carry out the task on the memo.

Information for the students:

Students should be given the scenario as follows:

> Each group of students is a separate office in a large market research company. The tutor is both the chairperson of the company and (having plenty of time on his/her executive hands) also the mailing service.
>
> The company has been told that it is to conduct a programme of internal market research. The chairperson will issue a memo to each office requesting a brief report on a particular aspect of the company as a whole. Each office must then gather adequate, accurate and appropriate information to produce that report by the sole means of written communication with the other offices. This is the only channel of communication allowed. When a group has collected all the required information it is to transmit it to the chairperson in the form of a brief written report.
>
> Offices indicate that they have mail to be delivered by raising their hands, whereupon it will be collected by the mail service and delivered.

THE INITIAL MEMORANDA

To: *Office A*
From: *Chairperson*
Date: 25/2/86   Re: *Internal Consumer Research*

In view of our company's recent decision to construct a complete consumer profile of its employees please prepare a brief report on the magazines and papers read by employees in the past two years. This should reach me as soon as possible.

To: *Office B*
From: *Chairperson*
Date: 25/2/86   Re: *Internal Consumer Research*

In view of our company's recent decision to construct a complete consumer profile of its employees please prepare a brief report on the drinks and beverages habitually consumed by our employees. This should reach me as soon as possible.

37

To: *Office C*
From: *Chairperson*
Date: 25/2/86   Re: *Internal Consumer Research*

In view of our company's recent decision to construct a complete consumer profile of its employees please prepare a brief report on snacks and sweets habitually consumed by our employees. This should reach me as soon as possible.

To: *Office D*
From: *Chairperson*
Date: 25/2/86   Re: *Internal Consumer Research*

In view of our company's recent decision to construct a complete consumer profile of its employees please prepare a brief report on the types of books read by employees and the frequency of reading. This should reach me as soon as possible.

To: *Office E*
From: *Chairperson*
Date: 25/2/86   Re: *Internal Consumer Research*

In view of our company's recent decision to construct a complete consumer profile of its employees please prepare a brief report on live and recorded music enjoyed by our employees. This should reach me as soon as possible.

To: *Office F*
From: *Chairperson*
Date: 25/2/86   Re: *Internal Consumer Research*

In view of our company's recent decision to construct a complete consumer profile of its employees please prepare a brief report on evening entertainments habitually enjoyed by our employees. This should reach me as soon as possible.

To: *Office G*
From: *Chairperson*
Date: 25/2/86   Re: *Internal Consumer Research*

In view of our company's recent decision to construct a complete consumer profile of its employees please prepare a brief report on television programmes habitually watched by our employees. This should reach me as soon as possible.

Supporting information for the tutor:

NOTES ON MEMORANDA

Precede the exercise with a lecture on written communication, covering report writing, letter writing and memo writing, so that the students have a clear idea of the difference of purpose and structure of the three forms of communication.

As the mail service collects and delivers the memo/report the tutor should use this opportunity to monitor the effectiveness and appropriateness of each communication and to exploit any ambiguity (eg delivering it to a different group if the address is imprecise; 'losing' it if both sender's and addressee's names are missing). The pressure exerted by using a brief class and demanding a rapid rate of communication tests group organization, information handling and the ability to design unambiguous and accurate written communication under pressure.

The exercise may well degenerate into chaos. If so it should be terminated before this goes too far, preferably when at least one group has submitted a report. Problems leading to this breakdown of communication illustrate many of the difficulties of hectic office life:

1. Hostility between groups
2. Imprecision/ambiguity in text
3. Imprecision/ambiguity in addressing
4. Problems of delay in receiving information
5. Problems when too much information arrives simultaneously
6. Filing problems (to keep or not to keep)
7. Group organization.

DISCUSSION NOTES ON MEMORANDA

A memo is a short note written for a particular purpose. It exists solely to get its purpose across. Usually it instigates an action or requires a decision or otherwise needs a response.

General rules:

1. The memo should always contain: date, sender's name, addressee, subject heading
2. The style should be simple and direct — no literary devices, gossip or introduction
3. The tone should be pleasant or neutral — hostility will annoy the addressee and prevent any response
4. The material should be arranged clearly on the page.

Behavioural rules:

1. Be selective — no polite chat, no introduction, only essential information

2. If longer than three sentences use space and numbering
3. Use a heading which clearly states the subject
4. Check the finished memo — make sure haste causes no errors.

Supporting bibliography and references:
Kirkman, John (1980) *Good Style for Scientific and Engineering Writing.* Pitman.
Deverell, C S (1973) *Successful Communication.* G Bell & Sons

Variations:

1. Ask students themselves to analyse their own behaviour, that of the other groups and the nature of the difficulties encountered. Use the plenary session to obtain suggestions for improving this type of communication.

2. Use the exercise as an introduction to intergroup communication to be followed by work on either report writing or group organization, such as exercises 2.1, 6.1, 6.2, 6.3 or 6.4.

3. Ask students to obtain copies of real memos from friends, relations or other teaching staff and to evaluate them. How much of the information in these memos is essential to the purpose of the memo?

■ Exercise 2.4

Applying for a job: preparation

Aims:

1. To encourage students to think about the education and training they are receiving;
2. To enable the students to share ideas about this education and training;
3. To encourage students to relate their education and training to the needs of employers.

Equipment and materials required:
Useful but not essential — overhead projector, OHP transparencies and pens (sufficient for number of students in class divided by four). Alternatively, a flipchart and felt pens may be used, depending on the class size and location.

Time required:
Approximately 35 minutes.

Procedure:
In stage 1 of this exercise, the class is divided into pairs and asked to discuss and make a note of their reasons for taking the course. After a few minutes, each pair should be joined with one other, and asked to compare their reasons. Each group is then asked to produce a list of reasons as to why an employer should employ someone from the course. In the final stage of the exercise, the tutor leads a discussion about the results of stages 1 and 2.

Information for the students:
The students should be given the following brief:

> STAGE 1 – In pairs (3-5 minutes):
> (a) Why are you taking this course?
>
> STAGE 2 – in fours (10 minutes):
> (b) Share the reasons given in (a).
> (c) Discuss reasons why an employer should employ someone from this course.
> (d) Keep a record of your reasons discussed in (c).
>
> STAGE 3 – Whole class (5 minutes):
> (e) Share reasons and discuss.

Supporting information for the tutor:
To keep the discussion moving around the class, ask for one or two ideas from each group in turn, until all the ideas are exhausted.

During the discussion of the reasons for taking the course, some students may express 'negative' reasons. A common one is 'I had no choice'. But of course they did have a choice – they could have taken a job that did not require qualifications, or they could have remained unemployed. For such students, try to elicit 'positive' reasons, eg 'I took this course because I wish to be employed as . . .'

As regards the reasons why employers should employ someone from the course, the following are some of the points that you could seek to elicit:

1. CONTENT OF THE COURSE

What are the benefits to the employer which result from the content of the course?

2. UNIQUE FEATURES

What does the course have that 'sets it apart' from many others? How does this benefit the employer?

3. METHOD OF LEARNING

What skills are being acquired as a result of the teaching methods employed (eg project work)? How do these skills benefit the employer?

Variations:

1. Combine the pairs to form larger groups (six or eight students) in stage 2.

2. *School variation (a)*

School pupils may have rather less choice about their current subjects than those in further and higher education. They may also be thinking in terms of higher education rather than employment or may, indeed, have no clear formulation of their intentions. This exercise may therefore be used to enable pupils to clarify their thinking on such matters.

For these reasons the exercise should be run either in respect of chosen subjects (rather than 'courses') or the school as a whole. Furthermore, it is best run as two successive or parallel exercises. One exercise will produce ideas on the subject area or school to be offered to an employer, and the other to produce ideas to be offered to a university, college or polytechnic. Either the class can be divided into two, each half being given one of these remits, or the whole class can carry out the exercise for employers and then repeat it for higher education.

3. *School variation (b)*

Pupils may not respond well to an employer-oriented exercise because one or more of the following apply:
(a) Local or national unemployment causes them to believe they stand no realistic chance of employment
(b) They are several years from completing their tuition
(c) The subjects they are studying have little direct vocational relevance.

A tutor may still want to carry out this exercise in the hope of overcoming some of these difficulties. However, a similar exercise can be run within a different scenario for analysing their education, such as publicizing the subjects or school, saving it from closure, persuading parents that it is a good choice or encouraging future pupils.

Similarly the exercise can be run as part of a pupil investigation of subjects they are not yet studying but wish to study in future years.

Related exercises: 1.2 and 5.5

Exercise 2.5

Writing a curriculum vitae and a covering letter

Aims:

1. To encourage students to think about the value of their education, qualifications, experience and other qualities;
2. To encourage the students to think about how these relate to the requirements of employers;
3. To give the students practice in presenting information about themselves in an effective manner.

Equipment and materials required:
Sufficient copies of job descriptions for the whole class.

Time required: (minimum 40 minutes)
Approximately 35 minutes of class time, plus 60 to 90 minutes of the students' own time.

Procedure:
In stage 1 of this exercise, the students complete a curriculum vitae. In stage 2, the class is divided into pairs to compare and discuss their CVs. They are asked to identify their main 'selling features' in relation to a specified job advertisement, and to make a note of these. Each of these features is then to be converted into a suitable form of words for inclusion in a covering letter.

In the third stage of the exercise, the tutor leads discussion about the results of stage 2. The students then individually complete a covering letter to accompany their CV.

Information for the students:
The students should be given the following brief:

STAGE 1 – Individually:

(a) Complete a curriculum vitae, paying particular attention to the overall presentation.

STAGE 2 — In pairs (20 minutes):

(b) Compare CVs, and discuss strengths and weaknesses in relation to the job advertisement provided.

(c) For each of you, identify one of your strengths in each of these sections: academic qualifications; other qualifications; work experience; interests.

(d) Express each of these strengths in a form of words suitable for a covering letter.

STAGE 3 — Whole class (15 minutes):

(f) Share results of 2(d), and discuss.

STAGE 4 — Individually:

(g) Complete a covering letter to accompany your CV, applying for the job advertised.

The students will require lectures or guided discussions on writing a curriculum vitae and on writing a covering letter. They will also require a suitable job advertisement to be used in stages 2 and 4.

Supporting information for the tutor:
In the lecture/discussion on how to write a curriculum vitae, students should be encouraged to use suitable 'labelled' sections, and to use horizontal and vertical space to make the CV attractive and readable. One possible example, showing the type of information required, is given below.

In the covering letter, students should be encouraged to do the following:

1. Give the job title and reference.
2. State where and when the job was seen.
3. Refer to your enclosed CV.
4. Highlight your main strengths (or 'selling points').
5. Reinforce your suitability for the job.
6. State when you will be available for interview.

Typical example of a curriculum vitae:

PERSONAL DETAILS

Name:	Mary BLOGGS
Marital Status:	Single
Age:	19
Date of Birth:	26th January 1965

Home Address: 958 Abbeydale Road South
                 Sheffield S7 2XX
                 Tel: 0742 364137

EDUCATION

1970-76   Abbeydale Primary School, Sheffield

1976-83   Carterknowle Comprehensive

1983 to date   Sheffield City Polytechnic

ACADEMIC QUALIFICATIONS

1981   GCE O levels: English Language (B), Art (A),
                French (A), History (C), Mathematics (B),
                Physics (B), Geography (C).

1983   GCE A levels: Economics (B),
                Mathematics (C), History (C).

In 1985:   Higher Diploma in Financial Sector Studies

OTHER QUALIFICATIONS

                Clean driving licence (since September 1983);
                Conversational knowledge of French;
                Ability to program in BASIC and operate
                WORDWISE wordprocessing package.

WORK EXPERIENCE

1982   Voluntary work for 'Help the Aged', assisting
                with fund-raising events and helping in Knowle
                Old People's Home (July-September).

1983   Shop assistant in Woolworths, Sheffield
                (July-September).

INTERESTS AND HOBBIES

                Walking and backpacking, hostelling, attending
                the theatre, badminton, dressmaking.

MEMBERSHIP OF CLUBS AND SOCIETIES

                Youth Hostels Association (Secretary of
                Carterknowle YHA Group);
                British Trust for Conservation Volunteers;
                Crucible Club;
                Carterknowle Badminton Club.

REFEREES

Mr S Henshaw BA MPhil DipEdTech
Principal Lecturer
Department of Accountancy Studies
Sheffield City Polytechnic
Pinder Lane
Sheffield S1 4AB

Mr P Harmley
26 Totley Hall Lane
Sheffield S17 4AB

Signed:

Date: 16 November 1984.

Supporting bibliography and references:
Bufton, I, Aram, J and Roberts, L (1983) *Applications and Interviews.* AGCAS Careers Information Booklet. Central Services Unit for University and Polytechnic Careers and Appointments Services (CSU).
Stanton, N (1982) *The Business of Communicating.* Pan.

Variations:

1. Combine the pairs to form groups of four in 2(d).

2. Form groups of four at the beginning of stage 2.

3. *School variation (a)*
If CV writing is inappropriate for your pupils, the same general objectives can be attained using a similar structure if the exercise is built around an UCCA application form or similar. Alternatively you may prefer to concentrate simply on those sections of CVs and applications which are generally under-used by applicants, namely the 'Interests' and 'Further Information' sections. Few applicants sell themselves effectively in these sections.

4. *School variation (b)*
An extended project can be constructed around this exercise. Pupils should prepare a CV or application form (which may even have been drafted by other students), complete it and undergo competitive interviews on the strength of it. A fuller version of such a structured course is given in Section C.

Exercise 2.6

Styles of language

Aims:

1. To sensitize students to different language styles;
2. To familiarize students with basic stylistic variables;
3. To encourage students to read texts critically.

Equipment and materials required:
One copy of the exercise sheet for each student; overhead projector or chalkboard for displaying results.

Time required: (minimum 45 minutes)
The exercise requires five minutes' briefing, 20 minutes for carrying out the exercise and 20 minutes for discussion.

Procedure:
Brief the class and issue the exercise sheets. Students should be paired off and each pair should take the list of different styles of language and plot them on a simple xy graph. The x axis of the matrix should represent the degree of formality of the text while the y axis represents the degree of factuality. When finished, all graphs should be combined into one overall class graph.

Information for the students:
Briefing:

> The following is a list of various styles of language. Draw a graph with x and y axes scaled 0 to 100. The x axis should record the degree of formality in the style and the y axis the degree of factuality in the style. If there are any styles which are hard to position, what is difficult about them? In plotting the position of each text try to decide where the essays and reports you usually write would fit. What types of text are they most like?

HANDOUT – STYLES OF TEXT

1. TV news
2. Telephone directory
3. Radio advertisement
4. Editorial in the *Guardian*
5. Editorial in the *Sun*
6. TV advertisement
7. TV weather report
8. Fairy story

9. Social security leaflet
10. Song lyric
11. Letter to a relative
12. Intimate talk with boy/girlfriend
13. Parent telling off child
14. Lecture on computing
15. Valentine card
16. Science fiction novel
17. Political speech
18. Sports commentary
19. Manual for a microcomputer
20. Shakespearian drama
21. Knitting pattern
22. Swearing
23. Recipe
24. *The Beano*
25. Train timetable
26. Memorandum
27. Letter to bank manager
28. Conversation at a party.

Supporting information for the tutor:
This will give a scattergram of the styles which show a degree of correlation between factuality and formality, but not a clear one-to-one correspondence. Discussion should be used to draw out the reasons behind the positioning of texts on the matrix. This can be done by plotting the average of class decisions on a master graph on chalkboard or OHP. In cases of wide disagreement, plot a line or circle to encompass the area of uncertainty. Ask for judgements on each text in turn and obtain justifications from any pair of students offering deviant descriptions. When the master graph is complete plot each pair's ideas on their own reports and discuss the variation of extremes. Any texts which appear problematic for one reason or another should be explored in detail. If the axes of formality and factuality seem irrelevant in defining the style of a particular kind of text, then discuss those criteria which should yield more meaningful distinctions.

Supporting bibliography and references:
Kirkman, John (1980) *Good Style for Scientific and Engineering Writing.* Pitman.
Vardaman, George (1970) *Effective Communication of Ideas.* Van Nostrand Reinhold.

Variations:

1. If there are particular styles of text which the students are expected to produce or understand, these should be included in the list.

2. Students can be asked to think up their own lists of 20 styles of text and then the lists of texts can be exchanged between pairs. Alternatively, collections of texts can be created by tutor or students which can be used as the basis for assessment.

Exercise 2.7

Readability and style

Aims:

1. To give students a simple model of stylistic variation;
2. To show that the style of a text affects the degree of comprehension of its subject by readers;
3. To encourage students to use simple constructions in their own writing.

Equipment and materials required:
A watch with a second hand or a stop watch. One copy of each of the three texts for each student. A copy of the question and answer sheet for the tutor. Pens, paper and chalkboard or overhead projector.

Time required: (minimum 60 minutes)
Five minutes will be required for the briefing. Students will require one and a half minutes to read each text plus a breathing space of about two minutes, and five minutes to answer the questions. Discussion and calculation of results takes about 20 minutes, depending on the size of the class, and the final plenary session requires about 15 minutes.

Procedure:
Brief the students. Describe the task to the class and then issue one copy of each of the texts to each student, face down. For each text carry out the following procedure:

1. Give the students one and a half minutes to read the text. Time this as precisely as possible.

2. When the time has elapsed students must turn the texts face down. A minute or so should be given for the text to be forgotten. If desired, rehearsal can be prevented by asking the class to count backwards in threes from 200, a task of sufficient complexity to prevent most people from thinking about the text they have just read.

3. Ask each of the five questions associated with the text and students must write down 'Y' or 'N' for their answers. Ensure that the questions are answered with regard to the text rather than the students' own knowledge. Insist that they write down something for each question even if they do not believe they know the answer.

4. When all five questions have been asked, go on to the next text.

When all three texts have been treated in this manner collect the answer sheets. Tell the class that the sheets represent their level of understanding of each of the texts. Now they are to assess the readability of each text. They should form pairs and rank the three texts in order of readability. Although this is an intuitive judgement it is presumably based on features in the texts. Therefore, each pair should also list those features in the text which make it more or less readable.

Meanwhile the tutor adds the number of correct answers for each text. The tutor should then gather the collective opinion of the readability of the three texts and record this on the chalkboard. He/she will find that most students think text 3 is most readable, text 2 least readable and text 1 in the middle, though a small minority of students may disagree. Against each text write the number of correct answers. On every occasion on which we have run this exercise the highest number of correct answers is obtained for text 3 and the lowest for text 2.

Although there is little point in conducting statistical tests on the results, because the exercise is not a controlled experiment, point out that random answers for a given text should equal:

$$\frac{\text{number of students in the class}}{2} \times 5$$

So 20 students should give a random result of 50 correct answers. It is the difference between this expected random figure and the actual result which shows how much learning has taken place. Often text 2 is close to random and text 3 has answers between 20 and 50 per cent above random predictions.

Finally, discuss the features that make texts readable (hence comprehensible) and demonstrate the readability formula.

Information for the students:

TEXT 1

'Ambiguity' is itself an ambiguous term. It can mean mere confusion, used when the writer does not know or understand the text under consideration. It can mean multiplicity of meaning, under the assumption that the number of possible meanings is finite and intended. Or it can mean 'possessing a large number of meanings' where the number of interpretations are many but each one is clear. It can also be found at all levels of language, from sound and spelling through words to syntax and semantics. One word may have different denotations or connotations, a sentence may change its meaning according to the context in which it is found, phonemes will be heard differently according to the prevailing dialect of the hearer. In general writers use the word 'ambiguity' ambiguously, seldom stating which of its senses is intended.

TEXT 2

Furthermore we should not believe that anaphora is restricted merely to reference to other items within the text in which it occurs. We can distinguish endophoric anaphora and exophoric anaphora, in addition to cataphora (which some would argue is a form of anaphora). Endophoric anaphora involves explicit reference, through pronouns or partial repetition, to other linguistic items in the same text, whereas exophoric anaphora refers to items outside the text. Cataphora is reference forward to items not yet mentioned as opposed to anaphora which, notwithstanding its occasional use to encompass all forms of textual reference, strictly involves reference only to items previously mentioned. Anaphora is a necessary condition for cohesion though not necessarily sufficient to ensure coherence in a text.

TEXT 3

The smallest syntactic unit is the group. A group may consist of several words or only one. If there are more than one then one of them will be the headword. This is the keyword, the most important word in a group. Headlines usually reduce groups to their headwords. For example the sentence 'Three ruthless robbers violently stole 200 valuable jewels from a High Street jewellers' might be reduced to 'Robbers Steal Jewels'. Groups can often be replaced by pronouns. In such a case the headword determines the pronoun used. For example, 'they' would replace 'robbers' which stands for 'three ruthless robbers'. In a similar way the headword of the subject determines whether the verb is singular or plural.

Supporting information for the tutor:
Questions to ask:

Read each question slowly, but only read it once.

TEXT 1

1. Can 'ambiguity' mean 'confusion'? (Yes)
2. Does one meaning of 'ambiguity' assume that the number of possible meanings is finite? (Yes)
3. Are there any levels of language which are unambiguous? (No)
4. Do writers usually use the term 'ambiguity' unambiguously? (No)
5. Does dialect cause ambiguity? (Yes)

TEXT 2

1. Does exophoric anaphora refer to texts? (No)
2. Is anaphora a form of cataphora? (No)
3. Can partial repetition be a form of endophoric anaphora? (Yes)
4. Does anaphora ensure coherence? (No)
5. Does exophoric anaphora refer to other linguistic items? (No)

TEXT 3

1. Can one word be a group? (Yes)
2. Is the headword the word left out of a headline? (No)
3. Can a group be replaced by a pronoun? (Yes)
4. Does the pronoun determine the headword? (No)
5. Can the headword of the subject determine if a verb is plural? (Yes)

Discussion notes on readability:
When all the calculations have been done you should find that there is a correlation between the comprehension shown for each text, the intuitive assessment of the text and the readability index for the text. The index is solely based on the average length of words in the text and the average length of the sentences in a text. The longer each is, the more unreadable is the text. The formula used here produces a resulting number which notionally correlates with USA grades of reading. In a crude way the readability index gives a 'reading age' for each particular text, although this takes no account of content.

The readability formula used here is derived from work by the Americans, J Peter Kincaid and Leroy J Delionbach:

$$\text{INDEX} = 0.5 \times \frac{\text{average words}}{\text{sentence}} + 4.71 \times \frac{\text{average letters}}{\text{word}} - 21.43$$

Text	No of sentences	No of words	No of letters	Average wds/sent	Average lets/wd	Index
1	7	136	678	19.4	4.98	11.73
2	5	120	677	24	5.64	17.13
3	10	120	583	12	4.86	7.46

Discussion will show that characteristics other than word and sentence length affect readability, but paying attention to these alone is sufficient to improve understanding. Other features which affect readability and should be included in discussion are:

1. Passives
2. Abstract nouns
3. Auxiliary verbs and complex tenses
4. Dependent clauses
5. Punctuation
6. Relative clauses
7. Familiarity of subject matter
8. Familiarity of vocabulary
9. Use of examples
10. Completeness of text.

Supporting bibliography and references:
Kirkman, John (1980) *Good Style for Scientific and Engineering Writing.* Pitman.
Kincaid, J Peter and Delionbach, Leroy J (1973) Validation of the automated readability index: a follow-up. *Human Factors*, 15(1), pp.17-20.

Variations:

1. Students can be asked to perform the calculation of the index themselves to encourage them to use the formula as a rough guide to their own writing style.

2. Students can be given a project to design a computer algorithm/program or a mechanical scheme of human assessment for determining readability involving such steps as 'Count the number of abstract nouns'. When the topics of word and sentence length are raised discuss the various meanings of the word 'length' (syllables, phonemes, stresses, clauses, groups and topics can all be used as units of length) and ask them to devise their own readability index.

3. The readability index can be applied to a number of 'found' texts, such as the texts used in exercise 2.7 or 7.4, to explore the nature of stylistic variation.

4. *School variation*

Pupils might be encouraged to compile a collection of texts which they regard as having different levels of readability. When they have ten or more texts they can be ranked on intuitive grounds from 'most readable' to 'least readable'. The readability formula can then be used to test this intuitive ranking. Where the formula gives a ranking significantly different from the pupils' intuitive ranks, hold a discussion and perhaps a deeper analysis of the problem text to establish reasons for the initial intuitive judgement.

■ Exercise 2.8

Some common problems in written communication

Aims:

1. To encourage students to consider common types of written error;
2. To show that recognizing an error does not necessarily mean being able to describe or correct it;
3. To introduce students to the idea of ambiguity in written texts and the corresponding need for precision and clarity;
4. Optionally, as an introductory exercise, to enable group operation on a simple task.

Equipment and materials required:
A copy of the problem sheet for each student and chalkboard or OHP to display results.

Time required: (minimum 45 minutes)
Approximately five minutes will be required for the briefing. Allow about 20 minutes for detecting the errors and a further 20 minutes for plenary discussion of the results.

Procedure:
Divide the class into small groups or pairs. Give each student a copy of the problem sheet. Ask each group to carry out the following three tasks for each of the ten texts on the sheet:

1. Locate the problem or problems in each text.
2. Explain the nature of the problem(s).
3. Rewrite the text so that the problem is removed.

A plenary session should then be held in which:

1. Groups who have identified and solved problems explain them to those who have not.
2. The problems are categorized into types.
3. Generalizations are extracted about the avoidance of such problems and advice on correcting them.

Information for the students:
Students should be encouraged to debate possible errors in the texts as experience shows that some features may or may not be errors. They should also try to improve each text as much as possible and to look for possible general categories of problem.

Supporting information for the tutor:

NOTES ON PROBLEMS IN WRITTEN COMMUNICATION

These notes consist firstly of the problem sheet to be given to students, then a text-by-text commentary on the problems. The texts are all actual quotations from commercial newspapers and magazines.

PROBLEM SHEET

1. Mr and Mrs Simon Parker request the honour of your presents at the marriage of their daughter Eve to Mr James Turner.

2. Dear Mum,
   Just a card to say I arrived alrite and if you don't know my address write and arsk me for it and I will send it to you.
   Love, Alfie.

3. INSTRUCTIONS
   Pour a teaspoonful of shampoo into the palm of each hand.

4. 100 New Price Rises
   But grocers say they will not hit housewives.

5. Elizabeth found herself on a stool by the nursery fire. Securely pierced by a long brass toasting-fork she held a square piece of bread to the glowing flameless fire.

6. I take back, with the greatest regret, the libellous remarks I made about Mrs Anne Cherry.

7. POLICE FOUND SAFE UNDER BLANKET

8. When deployed section commanders were apt to shoot themselves instead of seeing that their men understood the Fire Orders.

55

9. To the question 'In general do you approve or disapprove of Mr Johnson as President' 72 per cent of those asked replied 'Yes' and 26 per cent 'No'.

10. Had it not been for the so-called 'die-hards' — a term so often referred to us Nationalists disparagingly, yet so invigoratingly to those who do not betray principles — who have unfailingly sustained the European theory of our now muddled thinking on 'European theory' of our ethnological existence, by now muddled thinking on this subject would have been more general and deep-rooted.

NOTES

All the texts illustrate one or more forms of ambiguity or imprecision. They can be used to illustrate the point that the term 'ambiguity' is itself highly ambiguous.

1. Not a misspelling but wrong choice of one of two homophones. Specific cultural knowledge tells us that 'presents' are expected at a wedding but not requested.

2. Misspelling of 'alrite' and 'arsk' based on phonological rules, a common error of those unused to writing as in the common supposition that 'could have' is written 'could of'.
   False presuppositions: syntax can be correct even if the resulting sentence does not refer to a possible state of events.

3. A physical impossibility resulting from the belief that instructions must be clear if they are in simple language. To be clear, instructions must also detail all necessary stages of a process. For technical students it is useful to draw the parallel with algorithms and/or computer programs.

4. Ambiguous anaphora: 'they' could refer to prices or grocers. All pronouns are necessarily ambiguous so reference must be clarified. Illustrate this in class by using several sentences with the word 'it' in them.
   Semantic ambiguity: 'hit' could mean 'affect' or 'punch'. Be aware of multiple meanings, including colloquialisms.

5. Textual ambiguity — how are the two sentences connected? What is 'securely pierced'? Discuss the placing of clauses and word groups. A dependent group should be as close as possible to the noun or group it depends upon.

6. Clausal ambiguity. The reader must understand that 'regret' applies to something unstated rather than what is stated. Cultural knowledge of the contexts of libellous statements and their consequences tell us that you say you regret the libel even if you mean that you regret that you have to say that you regret it.

7. One word has two possible syntactic functions — 'safe' could be a noun or an adjective. One word has two possible tenses — 'found' could be active past or passive. These would be disambiguated by function words. Discuss the ambiguity of headlines consequent on the removal of function words. Ask students to list all the function words in problem 10.

8. Phrasal ambiguity because of omitted 'for'. Is 'shoot' transitive or intransitive? Discuss idioms such as 'feel yourself' and 'help yourself' and phrasal verbs.

9. Mismatched question and answer. Yes/no answers presuppose a single proposition in the question. Relate the discussion to question structuring (eg exercise 4.2). Also the results do not add up to 100 per cent.

10. An example of overlong structures leading to complex expression and proof-reading errors. Could improve paragraphing, punctuation, length of sentences, clarity of thought, use of cliché. Relate this to exercise 2.8.

DISCUSSION NOTES ON WRITTEN PROBLEMS

These texts bring home to technical students the imprecision of normal language in comparison with the technical vocabulary of their preferred discipline. The exercise can be used prescriptively by advising on actions to avoid, as a general exhortation to avoid imprecision and to encourage re-reading and editing of reports and essays, as an assessment or as an entry point into wider discussion of the syntactic and semantic structures of language.

Emphasis can be laid on the ambiguity of most natural language and the consequent need for clear statement of presuppositions and context.

Supporting bibliography and references
Cooper, Bruce (1964) *Writing Technical Reports*. Penguin.
Kirkman, John (1980) *Good Style for Scientific and Engineering Writing*. Pitman.

Variations:

1. Ask students to follow up the exercise by collecting examples of similar ambiguity from their reading and conversation. These collections can then be used as the basis of further discussion.

2. *School variation*
   In some school contexts and possibly in the more general communication courses in further education this exercise can be used to begin a discussion of creativity or humour. Point out that most of the texts seem funny because they have more than one meaning. Explore the notion that humour arises from a creative combination of two or more ideas. Ask pupils to produce texts which combine two or more meanings and judge their creativity and humour. Ask pupils to discover if some forms of linguistic ambiguity are more likely to be humorous than others.

■ **Exercise 2.9**

Ambiguity in texts

Aims:

1. To give students practice in critical reading;
2. To encourage students to evaluate their own writing;
3. To give students practice in clear writing;
4. To illustrate the necessary ambiguity inherent in most texts;
5. To demonstrate the value of a work study pair/group.

Time required: (minimum 20 minutes)
The exercise requires about two minutes for briefing and about 20 to 30 minutes to carry out, including a brief plenary session.

Procedure:
Brief the students. Ask them to prepare their paragraphs. When each student has written a paragraph he/she must exchange it with a neighbour and must then attempt to discover any ambiguities and/or imprecisions in the paragraph. After ten minutes the two students should compare results. A plenary session can discuss the nature of the ambiguities found.

Information for the students:
   You are to write a paragraph of about 100 words on some aspect

of the subject you are studying. The paragraph you write and every sentence within it must be totally unambiguous.

When you have written an unambiguous paragraph you will exchange it for that of your neighbour. You should examine his/her attempt and try to find ambiguities and imprecisions in it. He/she will be doing the same to yours. Note any ambiguity you find together with the possible meanings you think it may have.

Finally, after ten minutes' evaluation, compare results. Explain to each other why you think the sentences/text are ambiguous and try to resolve the problems you have both found.

Supporting information for the tutor:

Students should be encouraged to discover ambiguity of any and every kind. The exercise can be used as a general introduction to the problems of writing before working on more detailed exercises such as exercise 2.8.

In the plenary session ask students to describe the ambiguities they have found and why they are difficult to avoid. Where students cannot agree about a particular phrase or sentence get the rest of the class to resolve the debate.

Variations:

The pairs established by this exercise could become the basis of work study groups. It is often useful practice for students to have another student or group of students who will mutually oversee and evaluate work without hostility or pressure. This exercise can be used to establish the principle and the value of such mutual criticism. The tutor should decide whether to establish such study pairs or study groups on a formal basis or simply to suggest the possibility to a class, depending on the degree of initiative shown by students in other exercises.

Topic 3: Oral presentation

Exercise 3.1

Giving instructions

Aims:

1. To introduce students to some of the problems of giving instructions;
2. To demonstrate the importance of being explicit and of carefully structuring instructions;

59

3. To demonstrate the importance of feedback in effective communication.

Equipment and materials required:
Mobile blackboard and chalks (or flipchart, stand and felt pens).

Time required:
Approximately 15 minutes.

Procedure:
One student is asked to stand facing the mobile blackboard so as to be hidden from the rest of the class. On this blackboard is drawn a simple diagram. The student is asked to 'instruct' the rest of the class as to how to draw this diagram. Without any questioning or discussion, the rest of the class attempts to draw the diagram from the student's instructions. When the description is completed, the students compare their drawings with the original. This procedure is repeated three or four times with other students as 'instructors' using different drawings.

In stage 2 of the exercise, the same basic procedure is followed, but this time the class is allowed to ask the 'instructor' a limited number of questions. This procedure is then repeated three or four times.

The class is then divided into small groups for stage 3 of the exercise. Each group is asked to produce a set of guidelines on giving instructions. These guidelines are then shared in a class discussion.

Information for the students:
Each student 'instructor' will require a different diagram. All that is required in each case is an arrangement of simple shapes, as shown in Figures 1 and 2.

Supporting information for the tutor:
Some of the guidelines which should emerge in discussion are:

1. Try to create the appropriate expectations in the listener, ie state how you are going to tackle the task;
2. Try to think about the task from the listener's point of view;
3. Break the instructions down into simple steps;
4. Use 'signposts' to let the listener know what you are going to do next;
5. Periodically summarize what you have said so far;
6. Emphasize the main points, repeat if necessary;

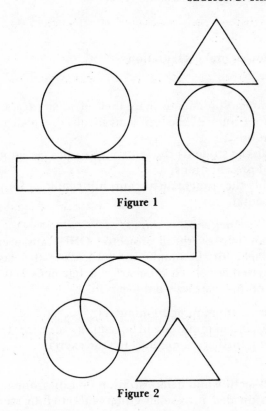

Figure 1

Figure 2

7. Use as many channels of communication as possible;
8. Encourage feedback;
9. Proceed with the instructions at a speed determined by the ability of the listener to comprehend;
10. Use simple language.

Supporting bibliography and references:
Stanton, N (1982) *The Business of Communicating.* Pan.

Variations:

1. Divide the class into pairs and allow each pair to work out a strategy before playing the role of 'instructor'.

2. Divide the class into small groups and allow each group to work out a strategy. One student from the group then acts as 'instructor' for that group.

3. After discussion of the guidelines, repeat the exercise using the method described in (2), and using more complicated diagrams.

61

■ Exercise 3.2

Preparing for an oral presentation

Aims:

1. To encourage students to share their ideas and fears, and to think about some of the problems involved in giving oral presentations;
2. To enable the students to identify strategies for improving their oral presentations;
3. To provide the students with a useful technique for preparing oral presentations.

Equipment and materials required:
Lecture materials, overhead projector, OHP transparencies and pens (sufficient for the number of students in the class divided by four). Alternatively, a flipchart and felt pens may be used, depending on the class size and location.

Time required: (minimum 40 minutes)
Approximately ten minutes will be required for the introductory lecture, and a further 30 minutes for the exercise.

Procedure:
After a brief lecture and demonstration on using 'brain patterns', the class is divided into small groups (about four students per group). Each group is asked to produce a brain pattern in preparation for a talk. After about 15 minutes, each group records its pattern on an OHP transparency and then presents it to the rest of the class for discussion.

Information for the students:
The students will require a lecture and demonstration on the use of brain patterns as a means of preparing, organizing, recording, storing and recalling information. The brief for the group exercise is as follows:

> Produce a 'brain pattern' in preparation for a 20-minute talk entitled 'The major factors involved in giving a talk'. After agreeing a suitable pattern, draw it on the OHP transparency provided, ready for class discussion.

Supporting information for the tutor:
Tony Buzan (1982) describes a useful way of setting down information so as to exhibit the relationships that exist between the various concepts. This technique of drawing 'brain patterns' can be used for a variety of purposes, one of

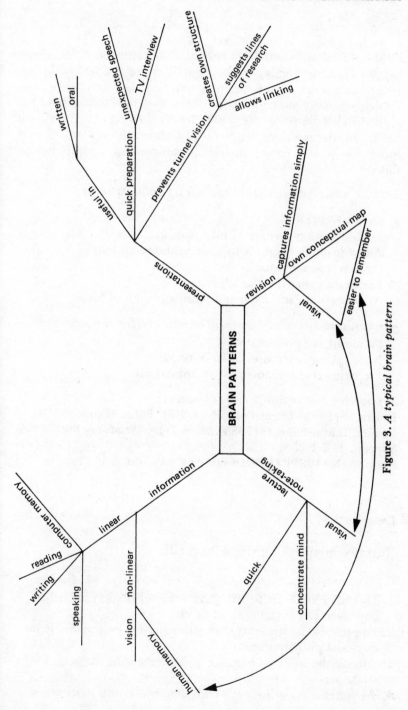

Figure 3. *A typical brain pattern*

these being to capture and organize the results of a 'brain-storming' session, as in this exercise.

Most students know the essential requirements for giving a talk. Their problems are not primarily due to a lack of knowledge. In preparing this brain pattern on 'Giving a Talk', the students usually make all the points that one would have included in a lecture on the topic. But by arriving at this position by group discussion rather than by lecture, the students are far more likely to change their behaviour when actually giving talks.

Lecture notes on the nature and use of brain patterns

1. BRAIN PATTERNS:
   Enable rapid recording of information;
   Allow interconnections to be seen and recorded;
   Prevent 'tunnel vision';
   Facilitate easier recall;
   Allow easy organization and reorganization of ideas.

2. USED FOR:
   Preparing for presentations;
   Note-taking in lectures or from books;
   Preparing revision notes for examinations.

Supporting bibliography and references:
Buzan, T (1982) *Using Your Head.* BBC Publications:
Palmer, R and Pope, C (1984) *Brain Train: Studying for Success.* E & F N Spon.
Stanton, N (1982) *The Business of Communicating.* Pan.

■ **Exercise 3.3**

'Just two minutes' — giving a short talk

Aims:

1. To enable students to recognize some of the key areas for improvement in giving short talks;
2. To provide the students with strategies for improving their own oral presentations;
3. To give the students practice in implementing these strategies;
4. To increase each student's confidence in giving short talks.

Equipment and materials required:
Video recorder, camera and playback facilities, overhead projector, OHP transparencies and pens, flipchart, felt pens, blackboard and chalk.

Time required: (minimum 60 minutes)
This depends on how many students actually give talks. You will require approximately six minutes per student, plus an additional 15 minutes' briefing and preparation time.

Procedure:
The students are told to prepare a two-minute talk. After about five minutes' preparation time, the talks are presented and recorded on video. When all, or the required number, of the talks have been recorded, they are replayed and discussed.

In stage 2 of the exercise, each student works on a particular aspect of his/her presentation. After five minutes of preparation time, each student gives part of the talk again to demonstrate the improvement made. It is not really necessary to record these repeat presentations.

Information for the students:
The brief at the start of the exercise is as follows:

> Prepare a short talk on any subject you wish, and then present this talk to the rest of the class. Your talk should last exactly two minutes. You have five minutes to prepare. While each student is presenting his/her talk, make a note of one good point about the presentation and one point which could be improved.

When the talks have been replayed, each student should be asked to revise one particular aspect of his/her talk, eg the opening, or the closing. Each student is then told to repeat the talk, or a sufficient part of it to demonstrate the improvement made.

Supporting information for the tutor:
In this exercise, it is very important not to undermine the self-esteem of the students. Thus, wherever possible you should emphasize good points about each talk, as well as mentioning those aspects which could be improved. Restrict the number of comments made about each talk to about four.

Although there are many details on which one could comment in analysing the talks, over the whole feedback session concentrate on making or eliciting the six main points listed below. For each talk, select one aspect which the student can improve easily and with maximum effect.

Notes on the six main points:

1. OPENING

   Must have impact, interest the audience and prepare them for what is to follow.

2. SIGNPOSTS

   'Point' the way through your talk using headings.

3. VISUAL AIDS

   Reinforce, explain and illustrate.

4. NOTES

   Short memory aids only. Key words on a small card.

5. POSITIVE ENERGY

   Transmit energy (enthusiasm) from a positive posture using positive language and gestures.

6. CLOSING

   Summarize and finish with a good strong close.

Supporting bibliography and variations:
Stanton, N (1982) *The Business of Communicating.* Pan.

Variations:

1. In stage 2, gather the students together into groups so that each group is working on one of the aspects listed. In this way the students can support one another and share ideas for improvement.

2. Instead of all students giving a presentation, some of the class can be given the role of 'observers'. This observer group can be asked to check for the aspects listed above. (This is useful if the class is a large one.)

3. If video-recording facilities are not available, use audio-recording, together with an 'observer group' as described in variation (2).

4. *School variation*
   As a means of encouraging pupils to develop some initiative

in researching a topic and to become aware of aspects of their subject that they may never otherwise encounter, ensure that each talk is on a different aspect of a taught subject area, but not something that has already been taught. The oral presentation can thus be built into a larger communications project and the relevant skills focused specifically on the student's academic subjects.

Exercise 3.4

The systematic approach to oral presentation

Aims:

1. To guide the students through a 'systematic approach' to the preparation of oral presentations;
2. To provide the students with checklists for improving their own oral presentations;
3. To give the students practice in implementing these strategies in the preparation and presentation of talks;
4. To increase each student's confidence in giving oral presentations.

Equipment and materials required:
Overhead projector, OHP transparencies and pens, flipchart, felt pens, blackboard and chalk.

Time required: (minimum two hours)
Allow approximately ten minutes' presentation time per group. In addition, you will require 80 minutes for briefing, preparation and self-evaluation, plus a few minutes for general discussion at the end of the exercise.

Procedure:
The class is divided into small groups (of about four or five students) and told to prepare a ten-minute talk. Each group is then guided through a 'systematic approach' in its preparation. At the beginning of each stage in this preparation, the groups are provided with sets of questions/instructions to focus their planning.

In stage 1, each group concentrates on defining the problem. In the next stage, they decide what the content is to be. Each member of the team then prepares his/her part of this main content. In stages 4 and 5 respectively, the introduction and

67

conclusion to the presentation are prepared. In stage 6, each group presents its talk to the rest of the class.

After all the talks have been given, each group is provided with the 'self-evaluation checklist' (shown in stage 7 below). When completed, these form the basis for the general class discussion about the exercise.

Information for the students:
The brief for the oral presentation is:

> As a representative group of students, you have been asked by the Students' Union to comment on the effectiveness of Freshers' Week. You will be allowed ten minutes for your group oral presentation.

Brief for students observing talks:

> While each group is presenting its talk, make a note of three good points about the presentation and three points which could be improved.

The brief for each stage of the exercise is as follows:

STAGE 1: PRELIMINARIES (10 minutes)

(a) Define your objectives: what do you want your audience to think or do as a result of your talk?
(b) Analyse your audience: what do you know about the background and attitudes of your audience (eg age, needs, motivation)?
(c) Consider the situation: what is the immediate situation (eg time, size of room, equipment, number in audience)?

STAGE 2: DECIDING THE CONTENT (15 minutes)

(a) Create a 'brain pattern' showing the content of your talk.
(b) Decide the main sections and structure of your talk.

STAGE 3: PREPARING THE CONTENT (30 minutes)

Each member of the team:
(a) Prepare a section of the talk.
(b) Write key words on a small card as 'memory joggers' for your section.
(c) Prepare visual aids.

STAGE 4: PREPARING THE INTRODUCTION (10 minutes)

(a) How will you 'hook' your audience? What will your first words be?
(b) What is the purpose of your talk?
(c) What benefit/value will your talk be for the audience?
(d) What action do you require from the audience?
(e) What are the main headings of your talk?

STAGE 5: PREPARING THE CONCLUSION (10 minutes)

(a) What are the main points to be reinforced in the summary?
(b) What is the final impression you wish to make? Do you want your audience to do anything?
(c) How will you close your presentation? What will your final words be?

STAGE 6: GIVING THE ORAL PRESENTATION (10 minutes)

STAGE 7: EVALUATING THE PRESENTATION (10 minutes)

(a) *Organization:*
Did the opening have impact?
Was the material sectioned, structured and signposted?
Did the closing 'round off' the presentation?
(b) *Material/content:*
Had you prepared appropriate notes?
Were the main ideas explained?
Was the amount of material/ideas correct?
(c) *Delivery:*
Was your voice clear and well-modulated?
Did your non-verbal behaviour enhance the presentation?
Were you lively and enthusiastic?
(d) *Visual aids:*
Were the visual aids clear and easy to see?
Were they appropriate for the ideas being expressed?
Did you present them effectively?
(e) *Relation to audience:*
Was the interest of the audience maintained?
Did you have eye contact with the audience?
Did you take account of feedback?

DID YOU ACHIEVE YOUR OBJECTIVES?

Supporting information for the tutor:
In this exercise, it is very important not to undermine the self-esteem of the students. Thus, wherever possible you should emphasize good points about each presentation, as well as mentioning those aspects which could be improved.

Although there are many details which one could comment on in analysing the talks, in the general discussion concentrate on reinforcing the six main points listed in the previous exercise.

Supporting bibliography and references:
Fisher, Cassie W and Constantine, T (1977) *Student's Guide to Success*. Macmillan.
Stanton, N (1982) *The Business of Communicating*. Pan.

Variations:

1. Stage 3 can be completed by the students in their own time.

2. Instead of all groups giving a presentation, some of them can be given the role of 'observers'. Each observer group can be asked to evaluate each presentation using the checklist in stage 7 above. (This is useful if the class is a large one.)

3. If video- or audio-recording facilities are available, and time allows, each group can review its own performance. This 'reviewing', together with the evaluation in stage 7, could be done by individual groups in a separate room, while other groups are still giving their talks.

4. The topic for the presentation could be:
   How to improve lectures.
   How to improve seminars.
   How the Students' Union could use microcomputers to streamline their administration.
   Or, a topic could be selected in one of the other subjects in the course.

5. *School variation*
   Use the variation note (3) from exercise 2.2 on p.35.

Related exercise: 2.2.

■ Exercise 3.5

A group talk on alternative energy

Aims:

1. To enable students to recognize some of the key areas for improvement in giving short talks;
2. To give the students practice in giving short talks;
3. To increase each student's confidence in oral presentation;
4. To introduce the students to the problems and advantages of working in groups.

Equipment and materials required:
Overhead projector, OHP transparencies and pens, flipchart, felt pens, blackboard and chalk.

Time required: (minimum two hours)
You will require 20 minutes for briefing and initial group preparation. The students can then research and prepare the material for the talk in their own time (about 40 minutes). Allow approximately ten minutes per group for the presentations,

and ten to 15 minutes for self-evaluation and general discussion at the end of the exercise.

Procedure:

The class is divided into small groups (of about four or five students) and told to prepare a ten-minute talk.

In stage 1, each group concentrates on defining the problem and deciding what the content is to be. Each member of the team then prepares his/her part of the presentation. In stage 3, each group presents its talk to the rest of the class.

After all the talks have been given, each group is provided with the 'self-evaluation checklist' (shown in exercise 3.4). When completed, these form the basis for the general class discussion about the exercise.

Information for the students:

The brief for the oral presentation is:

TALK ON ALTERNATIVE ENERGY

Elaskay, a large island off the west coast of Scotland, has been selected as the area to test the viability of an alternative energy programme. At this very early stage of planning, the governing body has decided to engage consultants to give short talks to groups of the 10,000 inhabitants of the island on various types of alternative energy. Clearly, the Elaskayans wish to know more about the various alternative sources of energy, how the energy is extracted and stored, the environmental and social implications, etc.

Your brief, as a team of consultants, is to prepare a short talk (ten minutes maximum) on one type of alternative energy.

The brief for each stage of the exercise:

STAGE 1: PRELIMINARIES (15 minutes)

(a) Analyse your audience: what do you know about the background and attitudes of your audience (eg age, needs, knowledge)?
(b) Consider the situation: what is the time allowed, size of room, equipment, number in audience, etc?
(c) Create a brain pattern showing the content of your talk.
(d) Decide the main sections and structure of your talk.
(e) Allocate one section for each member of the group to prepare.

STAGE 2: PREPARING THE CONTENT (10 minutes)

Each member of the team:
(a) Research and prepare your section of the talk.
(b) Write key words on a small card as 'memory joggers' for your section.
(c) Prepare visual aids.

STAGE 3: GIVING THE ORAL PRESENTATION (10 minutes)

(a) Each group gives its talk.

71

(b) While each group is presenting its talk, make a note of three good points about the presentation and three points which could be improved.

STAGE 4: EVALUATING THE TALKS (5 minutes)

(Use the evaluation checklist shown in exercise 3.4.)

Supporting information for the tutor:

In this exercise, it is very important not to undermine the self-esteem of the students. Thus, wherever possible you should emphasize good points about each presentation, as well as mentioning those aspects which could be improved.

Although there are many details which one could comment on in anlysing the talks, in the general discussion concentrate on reinforcing the six main points listed in exercise 3.3.

Supporting bibliography and references:

Fisher, Cassie W and Constantine, T (1977) *Student's Guide to Success.* Macmillan.

Stanton, N (1982) *The Business of Communicating.* Pan.

Variations:

1. Instead of all groups giving a presentation, some of them can be given the role of 'observers'. Each observer group can be asked to evaluate each presentation using the checklist above. (This is useful if the class is a large one.)

2. If video- or audio-recording facilities are available, and time allows, each group can review its own performance. This 'reviewing', together with the evaluation, could be done by individual groups in a separate room, while other groups are still giving their talks.

Related exercises: 1.1 and 6.1.

■ Exercise 3.6

Visual aids

Aims:

1. To enable students to practise the preparation of visual aids;
2. To give students practice in selecting aids for appropriate purposes;
3. To enable students to assess the efficacy of visual aids;

4. To make students aware of the factors affecting the success of visual aids.

Equipment and materials required:
Newspaper clippings, materials for the preparation of visual aids (eg blank OHP slides and pens).

Time required: (minimum 60 minutes)
The exercise requires about five minutes for briefing, 30 to 60 minutes for preparation of the aids and two minutes per student for presentation of the aids.

Procedure:
First, give a short lecture outlining the principles of visual communication, drawing attention to those features presenters should pay attention to. Give each student a newspaper story of about 200 to 500 words. Students should design a sequence of visual aids using the materials available which convey the information contained in the story as effectively as possible. When all students have created their visual aids they should be given two minutes to give their presentation. The presenter will only be allowed to use three spoken sentences in his/her presentation. All other information must be conveyed visually.

The remainder of the class should assess each presentation on its clarity, its brevity and its attractiveness. From the assessments discussion should result which establishes general principles of visual presentation.

Information for the students:
Briefing:

> You have been given a newspaper story which you are to present to the rest of the class using only three spoken sentences. All the rest of the information must be conveyed visually. You may use drawings, graphs, overlays, cartoons or any visual medium you feel appropriate. The tutor will supply you with materials for preparing these aids.

Supporting information for the tutor:
Students should be encouraged to think originally about the task in order to produce interesting and original material. Hint that non-verbal communication is a visual form of communication. In the class assessment of presentations ensure comment is made on the following:

REASONS FOR USING A PARTICULAR VISUAL AID:

1. To increase attention
2. To provide redundancy

3. To make information attractive
4. To summarize
5. To structure information
6. To provide continual reference for an audience
7. To express ideas that cannot easily be given verbally.

FEATURES OF THE DISPLAY:

1. Is the chosen display suitable for the information?
2. Was it shown too quickly?
3. Were colour, character size, graphics and underlining used appropriately?
4. Was the amount of preparation justified by the usefulness of the aid?
5. Was there too much information on display?

PRINCIPLES OF VISUAL PRESENTATION:

1. Information should be brief
2. Information should be simple
3. Information should be organized
4. Material should be varied wherever possible
5. Speech can be supported by aids other than blackboards/ OHPs such as non-verbal communication, three-dimensional models, overlays, computer graphics.

Supporting bibliography and references:
Bergin, F J (1976) *Practical Communication.* Pitman.
Deverell, C S (1973) *Successful Communication.* G Bell & Sons.
Wise, A and Wise, N (1971) *Talking for Management.* Pitman.

Variations:

1. If newspaper narratives are unsuitable for the course use short extracts from course textbooks.

2. If time is an important factor each presentation can be organized by groups of students with one aid being the responsibility of each student in the group.

3. The exercise can be included as part of a larger group exercise, eg a research project for which the results are to be presented in this way.

Exercise 3.7

Developing a point

Aims:

1. To enable students to practise developing and sustaining ideas in a presentation;
2. To give students practice in choosing appropriate methods for appropriate purposes in presentation;
3. To give students practice in specific rhetorical techniques.

Equipment and materials required:
A copy of the list of topics for development and a copy of the handout on techniques for each student.

Time required: (minimum 60 minutes)
The exercise requires about five minutes for briefing with about 20 minutes for each topic that is developed.

Procedure:
Decide on the number of topics students must develop. Three is sufficient to give practice without making the exercise tedious. Divide the students into pairs. Give each student the list of topics and ask each pair to choose topic(s) from the list and develop each using the methods given on the handout. They are to spend 15 minutes on each topic and then to compare results. A brief plenary session can be used to summarize the student's discoveries but this is unnecessary if the main aim is only to present the technique to the students.

Information for the students:
Briefing:

> You have been given a list of ten topics and a description of eight methods for developing those topics in a presentation. With your partner select a topic. Imagine you were to give a talk on that topic then carry out each of the short technical exercises for that topic. When you and your partner have both done this for a given topic compare results. Does one of you have a fuller list than the other? Did you both find the same approach yields the same kind of material? Did you both find all approaches equally easy to apply? Do they all yield useful material and, if not, why not? Will you be able to use this approach in other work?
>
> When you have identified those methods which seem most useful, remember them and make a deliberate point in using them next time you have to give an oral or written presentation.

LIST OF TOPICS:

1. The government is doing a difficult task well.
2. Microcomputers are nothing more than fashionable toys.
3. Rock music is artistic.
4. Language can be deceiving.
5. Sport is a waste of time.
6. It is necessary for a scientist or technologist to understand mathematics.
7. Predicting the future is not always uncertain.
8. The way people behave in pubs is artificial.
9. Lectures are not a good way of communicating.
10. Newspapers distort the truth.

TECHNIQUES FOR DEVELOPING AN IDEA

1. *Examples* — Write a list of four examples of the topic which can be used to illustrate it, to support it or to contradict it.
2. *Factual* — State a fact or statistic about the topic. If you know several relevant facts then list them all.
3. *Comparison* — Make a statement about the topic, then find a conflicting statement and compare the two. Which is most correct? Why?
4. *Anecdote* — Try to remember a personal anecdote or humorous story that is somehow related to the topic. Write it down. What point can it be used to illustrate?
5. *Visual aid* — Think of a visual aspect of the topic that could be demonstrated as part of a talk. Write it down. What would be the best way of presenting it?
6. *Rhetoric* — Take the topic and transform it in the following ways:
   (a) Exaggerate it
   (b) Understate it
   (c) Satirize or ridicule it
   (d) Directly contradict it
   (e) Invent a catchphrase or slogan which encapsulates it
   (f) Put the idea as briefly as you can
   (g) Think of a relevant quotation.
   (There are many other rhetorical devices which can transform the presentation of an idea.)
7. *Participation* — Think of some questions on the topic which you could ask your audience. Try to provide:
   (a) a factual question (eg who was it who devalued the pound?)

76

(b) an emotive question (eg do you want a society with four million unemployed?)

(c) a question which is very hard to answer because it has several aspects (eg is youth preferable to middle age?).

These can be used by you as a way of structuring your presentation. First ask the question then provide your own answers.

8. *Demonstration* — Is there some way that an aspect of your topic could be demonstrated (eg by a model, by taking the audience to a particular place, by setting up a simulation)? If so, write it down.

Supporting information for the tutor:
In the event of a plenary session try to establish answers to the following questions:

1. Which of the techniques were easiest and which hardest for each topic?
2. Which technique seems to stimulate thought most? Why do you think that is?
3. Do any methods seem appropriate to particular topics?
4. Do any methods seem appropriate for particular audiences?
5. Which devices are best for attracting audience attention?
6. Which devices are best for giving information?

Make the point that different people have different cognitive styles. Ways of thinking, in coming up with ideas, in presenting them and in processing and understanding them vary widely. The techniques in the exercise are only useful to the extent that they facilitate the production and presentation of ideas. If they prove restrictive or inappropriate for the audience they should be avoided.

Supporting bibliography and references:
Vardaman, George T (1970) *Effective Communication of Ideas.* Van Nostrand Reinhold.

Variations:

1. Replace the list of topics with a list drawn from the students' course or from exam papers.

2. Use the exercise as the starting point for actual oral present-ations. Each pair should choose one topic and develop points using the above methods, then organize that material into a five-minute presentation to the rest of the class.

3. Use the exercise as a way of evaluating the differences between written and spoken communication by exploring the usefulness of each device in a written context. Get the students to decide if there is an equivalent written or visual version of each device which could be used in an essay or report.

Topic 4: Interpersonal communication

■ Exercise 4.1

Introduction to interpersonal communication

Aims:

1. To introduce students to the ways of looking at interpersonal communication;
2. To encourage students to think about some of the skills required in face-to-face communication;
3. To encourage the students to think about how they might improve their interpersonal skills;
4. To enable students to gain experience of obtaining video-recorded feedback, and to overcome the 'cosmetic' effect of video.

Equipment and materials required:
Video recorder, camera and playback facilities.

Time required: (minimum 30 minutes)
Approximately ten minutes will be required for the briefing and preparation. Allow five minutes for the recording, replay and discussion of each 'interview' and a few minutes for concluding remarks at the end of the exercise.

Procedure:
This introductory exercise takes the form of a television 'chat show' interview. In the interview simulation, the students play the roles of both interviewer and interviewee. Thus, the class should be divided into pairs with one student in each designated as the television interviewer and the other as the 'guest'. The pairs are then given five minutes to prepare an interview on any topic they wish. The interview is to last exactly two minutes.

Each pair then conducts its interview in turn, while other members of the class observe. Give a non-verbal time signal after 90 seconds, and a countdown for the final ten seconds of each interview. After all the interviews have been recorded, they are replayed and discussed.

Information for the students:
For the simulation, students should be asked to 'be themselves' as much as possible. The brief for the exercise is as follows:

TELEVISION INTERVIEW

Complete this exercise in pairs.

1. You are to conduct an informal ('chat show'-type) interview in front of an audience.
2. One person is the 'television interviewer', the other person is the 'guest'.
3. Your interview can cover any topics you wish.
4. The interview must last exactly two minutes. You will be given a time signal after 90 seconds, and then a countdown for the final ten seconds.

Supporting information for the tutor:
Although this exercise deals with a particular kind of interpersonal interaction, viz. conducting an interview in public, the lessons to be learned from it can be applied to other situations. The overall problems addressed here are:

1. How can we ensure that the other person contributes to and enjoys the interpersonal communication?
2. How can we present ourselves more effectively?

In the opening stage of any interpersonal communication, it is important to establish a rapport with the other person. Thus, in this exercise the interviewers should show themselves to be courteous, warm and sincere, and should try to make the interviewee feel at ease and respected. However, because the responsibility for the interview rests with the interviewer, he/she often feels more nervous than the interviewee in this exercise. In the feedback and discussion session, it is useful to ask the students how they felt at particular points in the interviews. Their comments can usually be correlated with the non-verbal behaviour as seen in the video-replay.

It is important for the students to be aware of the two basic kinds of questions, viz. closed and open questions. The former are those to which there are really only one- or two-word answers. If the interviewer asks too many of these then he or she will have to work very hard in the interview, and the result is a rather unrewarding interaction. The latter, on the other hand, are 'open' in the sense that the interviewee is required to answer at greater length. Clearly, the interviewer should really be using 'open' questions much of the time, both to ensure an interesting interview and to relieve the 'pressure' on him/herself.

Having asked a suitable question and got the interviewee talking, the interviewer then needs to be able to keep him/her talking. This means being able to follow-up with questions or encouragement. It may be sufficient simply to remain silent, or to say 'yes' or 'mm' in a suitable tone. Other important ways of encouraging participation are by the use of eye contact, head nods, and other non-verbal signs of interest and agreement. Again, these should be noted on the video-replay when they are exhibited by the participants.

With regard to presenting oneself more effectively, the key here is to be positive. There are three main aspects to this which are useful for students to note. First, their body posture should be positive. This means being relaxed but alert; back held straight and not slouching; leaning towards the other person but not being aggressive. It is interesting to note the difference between the postures of the participants in each simulation interview. Very often, the interviewer (being more nervous and aware of the need to be in control) sits forward — attentive and 'ready-for-action'. The interviewee, on the other hand, will adopt a 'laid-back' posture. Appropriate positioning of the video camera can readily show which posture looks the more attractive.

Second, the nervous energy that so often 'leaks' out in unwanted non-verbal mannerisms and movements should be used effectively. Instead of trying to contain all this energy, it should be released as enthusiasm when talking, and as attentiveness when listening. While recording the interviews, note examples of distracting nervous behaviour and contrast it with examples of non-verbal behaviour which reinforce the message or image.

Third, think positively (about oneself, the other person, and the topic being discussed) and talk positively.

In the discussion after the simulations, it is very important to protect the self-esteem of the participants and generally to make them feel more confident. Thus, the emphasis should be on finding good points for each interview. Those points which are noted as requiring improvement should only be commented upon if it is actually possible for the person to improve them (and such points should be balanced by an equal number of good points). For each simulated interview, restrict comments to a few major items.

Over the whole discussion session, try to concentrate attention on the six main points noted below, and then reinforce these in the concluding remarks.

NOTES ON IMPROVING INTERPERSONAL COMMUNICATION

1. *Encourage participation*
   Use eye contact
   Ask open questions
   Reinforce participation using head nods, etc.

2. *Be positive*
   Adopt a positive posture
   Use nervous energy to project enthusiasm
   Think positively and use positive language.

Supporting bibliography and references:
Hargie, O, Saunders, C and Dickson, D (1981) *Social Skills in Interpersonal Communication.* Croom Helm.

Exercise 4.2

Questioning skills

Aims:

1. To make the students aware of the different kinds of questions;
2. To give the students practice in the skills of questioning.

Equipment and materials required:
Lecture materials.

Time required: (minimum 20 minutes)
About five to ten minutes will be required for the introductory lecture/discussion and briefing. The exercise then takes ten minutes followed by a few minutes' debriefing.

Procedure:
The class is divided into groups of three. In each group, one student is designated as the 'questioner', one as the 'respondent', and the other as an 'observer'.

To start the exercise, the questioner asks the respondent a closed question. After the response, the questioner than asks an appropriate open-ended question. At the end of this response,

81

the questioner encourages the respondent to continue by using a suitable follow-up. When the respondent has finished talking, the interaction is regarded as finished. The observer watches the whole interaction and discusses it with the participants at the end.

All this is then repeated with different students playing the roles, until each student has had the opportunity of playing the role of 'questioner'.

Information for the students:
The students will require a lecture/discussion on questioning skills, prior to the commencement of the exercise. For the simulation, students should be asked to 'be themselves', wherever possible. The brief for the exercise is:

QUESTIONING SKILLS

In groups of three:

1. Appoint one person as the 'questioner', one as the 'respondent' and one as an 'observer'.
2. The questioner asks the respondent a *closed question.*
3. The respondent answers.
4. The questioner then asks a suitable *open-ended question.*
5. The respondent answers.
6. The questioner then encourages the respondent to continue talking. This is achieved by using a suitable *follow-up* (eg asking for an example, illustration, justification, etc).
7. The respondent answers.
8. The observer leads a short discussion about the interaction.
9. Repeat steps (1) to (8) until each person has played the role of questioner.

Supporting information for the tutor:
The main purpose of this exercise is to give the students practice in formulating and asking different types of questions. Thus, before running the exercise it will be necessary to indicate the differences between closed and open-ended questions and follow-up prompts.

The distinction between closed and open-ended questions is one which most students recognize, and little more will need to be said than is given in the notes below. However, they may need more guidance on how to encourage the respondent to carry on talking after he/she has given an answer. For this, some kind of follow-up is required.

Sometimes all that is required to keep the respondent talking is a simple prompt such as 'Go on', or even silence. To guide the respondent into talking about some particular aspect of his/her answer, it is necessary to 'probe' in some way. One method of doing this is to repeat a keyword that the respondent has just uttered. Another, more explicit method, is to ask a 'probe question'. Thus, one might ask for an example, an illustration, justification, explanation, or clarification of what the respondent has just said. It is useful to ask the observers to make a note of the type of 'probe' (or other 'follow-up') used in the exercise.

Lecture/discussion notes on questioning skills:

1. CLOSED QUESTIONS

   These only require a one- or two-word answer by the respondent:

   (a) *Yes-no type*
       'Are you married?'
       'Are you in higher education?'
   (b) *Multiple-choice type:*
       'Are you at university, polytechnic, or college?'
   (c) *Identification type:*
       'What is your favourite colour?'

2. OPEN-ENDED QUESTIONS

   The answers can be any length, but usually require more than one sentence, eg 'Why did Manchester win the cup?'

3. FOLLOW-UPS

   Main types:
   (a) Simple prompt — 'Yes', 'Mmm'
   (b) Silence
   (c) Key word mirroring
   (d) Probe questions.

Supporting bibliography and references:
Hargie, O, Saunders, C and Dickson, D (1981) *Social Skills in Interpersonal Communication.* Croom Helm.

Variations:

1. Use video or audiotape recording to give feedback.

2. Where time allows, repeat the exercise after the class discussion.

3. Instead of giving a lecture/discussion on questioning skills, use exercise 4.1 as an introduction.

■ Exercise 4.3

Introduction to non-verbal communication

Aims:

1. To introduce students to the concept of non-verbal communication (NVC);
2. To show students how pervasive NVC is in everyday communication;
3. To enable the students to recognize the variety of non-verbal signals;
4. To encourage students to attend to the characteristics of their own non-verbal behaviour.

Equipment and materials required:
Facilities for small group discussion, paper and pencils.

Time required: (minimum 50 minutes)
Approximately ten minutes will be required for the briefing and preparation. Allow about 20 minutes for creating the lists and a further 20 minutes for comparison and discussion of the results.

Procedure:
Give a brief description of what is meant by a non-verbal sign. Arrange the students in small groups and ask each group to list 20 non-verbal signs and their meanings.

A plenary session should then be used to draw out some of the major characteristics of NVC.

Information for the students:
Students should be encouraged to pay attention to their own lives and behaviour to discover the signs they themselves use. They should also attempt to specify the meaning of each sign as fully as possible and to look for common features and categories in the lists they produce. The brief for the exercise is as follows:

NON-VERBAL COMMUNICATION

Complete this exercise in small groups.

1. You are to list 20 non-verbal signs in common use.
2. For each sign write down the meaning or meanings it can have. Be as precise as you can.
3. When you have a complete list write down any features which are common to several of the signs, such as the meaning they have or the part of the body being used.

Supporting information for the tutor:

NOTES ON NON-VERBAL COMMUNICATION

Some useful questions to provoke discussion are:

1. Do any of the listed signs have other meanings?
2. Can you think of other signs with the same meaning or function?
3. Do other people or cultures use different signs for any of these?
4. Which parts of the body are most frequently used in giving non-verbal signals? List all the signs you can think of for each part of the body you have mentioned.
5. What important personal or social meanings are not included here?
6. Are there any relationships between the sign used and the meaning it has?

Students are usually quick to realize that a list of 20 is very short. From this comes discussion of why NVC is so widespread and pervasive and why it exists when language is so versatile. In explaining this, notions such as 'redundancy', 'contradiction' and 'unconscious communication' are usually raised.

It is important that students recognize that some signs are virtually universal, such as the smile, and therefore probably of biological significance, but that most are learned and consequently arbitrary and culturally restricted. From this it follows that people can relearn NVC and can improve or alter their use of it. The examples of acting and teaching can be used to illustrate ways in which learned NVC is used to create complex meanings and to control the behaviour of an audience.

DISCUSSION NOTES ON NVC

The following categories of NVC should emerge from discussion:

1. *Bodily contact and touching behaviour.* Touching can express power relationships or familiarity. Different cultures permit different degrees of touching.

2. *Proximity.* The personal 'space bubble' differs from culture to culture, leading to problems of communication between, for example, British and Arabic businessmen. Students can observe the maintenance of the space bubble in seating behaviour on buses and in libraries.

3. *Bodily posture.* Body movement can be used to indicate interest/disinterest, eg in interviews.

4. *Head movement.* Used primarily for reinforcement in conversation. Nodding can encourage and head-shaking discourage people from talking.

5. *Facial expression.* Arguably the relics of animal ancestry and the most expressive aspect of NVC.

6. *Gesture.* Not only of hands and fingers but also other parts of the body, eg foot-tapping to indicate impatience.

7. *Gaze.* Eye contact regulates conversation and can indicate sexual interest.

8. *Vocal cues.* Emphasise that there are vocal signals which may not be verbal, such as grunts, laughter, cries.

9. *Appearance.* Dress, hairstyle, facial hair and personal adornment have their own codes and fashions.

Supporting bibliography and references:
Argyle, M (1967) *The Psychology of Interpersonal Behaviour.* Penguin.

Variations:

1. In multi-ethnic groups ask students from different cultures to give their equivalents for various non-verbal signs which have been discussed.

2. Use videos of interviewing, such as in exercise 4.1, to provide commentary on individual NVC.

3. If time allows, students can be given opportunity to practise specific signals before running an interview or oral present-ation exercise. Observers of the interview or presentation can be used to count the use of specific signs and note their effect on other participants.

Topic 5: Interviewing

Exercise 5.1

Information-gathering interviews

Aims:

1. To enable students to practise interviewing skills;
2. To sensitize students to the difficulties of information gathering by interview;
3. To give students practice in group organization and collective report writing.

Equipment and materials required:
One room for the interviews and one for the remainder of the class, briefing sheets, cassette recorder and cassettes.

Time required: (minimum four hours)
The exercise is run in three stages according to the brief given below. The first stage will require at least an hour for preparation. In the second stage allow between ten and 20 minutes for each interview depending on the size and number of the groups. In the third stage time must be given for the groups to design and prepare reports. This will depend on the length of report required. For a group of four students writing a report of about 1500 words at least half an hour should be given for the group debate and an hour for compilation of the report. Ideally students should be given a complete afternoon for this stage.

Procedure:
Divide the class into groups of four to six. There should be an even number of groups. Half of the groups become interviewing groups and half become observers. Each group is given a copy of the appropriate briefing. Each interviewing group must then design an interview to achieve the task while each observing group designs a scheme for observing and evaluating such an interview. Each interviewing group must carry out the following three tasks:

1. Design an interview to gather information with respect to the briefing.
2. Carry out the interview.
3. Compile and submit a group report based on the information obtained.

Each observing group must carry out three similar tasks:

1. Design a monitoring scheme with respect to the briefing below.
2. Carry out that scheme in observing one of the interviews.
3. Compile and present a report assessing the effectiveness of the interviewing group.

Information for the students:

BRIEFING FOR THE INTERVIEWING GROUPS

You are a consultancy team who have been called in by a communication department who wish to buy a microcomputer system. The department has £10,000 to spend and has no staff who are specifically trained in programming or computer science but several who have some general knowledge of computing. You must interview a representative of the department and prepare a report to be submitted to the department advising on the kind of system that would best meet the department's needs. This will only be a preliminary report of about 1500 words and there is no need to specify an exact system.

BRIEFING FOR OBSERVING GROUPS

You are to monitor an interview conducted by a trainee consultancy group who are assessing the needs of a communication department who wish to buy a microcomputer system. The firm who employs these consultants wishes to know:

1. How effective the interview is as a means of obtaining the necessary information;
2. How effective this particular group is in this particular task; and
3. How the group's performance might be improved.

Having observed the group in action in an interview you must prepare and submit a group report for the company of about 1500 words which gives the results of your observations.

Supporting information for the tutor:

The interviewee should be played by the tutor. He/she should present him/herself as reasonably ignorant of microcomputers, should be puzzled by technical jargon and should not volunteer information that the interviewers do not specifically request. Unless the students can be assumed to have some degree of knowledge of microcomputers it is advisable to make available reference sources on suitable equipment and/or preface the exercise with a library exercise on microcomputing. Groups should be allowed to record the interviews on cassettes.

Supporting bibliography and references:
Bergin, F J (1976) *Practical Communication.* Pitman.
Dineen, J (1977) *Talking Your Way to Success.* Thorsons.

Variations:

1. The exercise was designed for computing students. It can easily be tailored for students in other disciplines by altering the nature of the purchase and, if necessary, the purchasing institution.

2. The observing groups are used as a means of halving the necessary number of interviews and the time needed for the exercise. They can be omitted if the class is small or time is not a constraint.

3. The exercise can be run successfully as a full-day workshop. This is preferable to running several separate sessions as student attention can be concentrated on the exercise, the simulation appears more realistic and time is less of a constraint.

4. *School variation (a)*
   Schools may be unable to use two rooms simultaneously, in which case the interviews must be conducted either in some 'protected' part of the normal classroom or at some time outside the normal curriculum. Alternatively, if sufficient interviewees can be found to augment the tutor all interviews might be conducted simultaneously in a suitably divided room such as an assembly hall.

5. *School variation (b)*
   If it is thought that 'a communication department' is too remote from the pupils' or tutor's experience, computing facilities could be planned for any school section currently lacking them. It is interesting in particular to get science students to consider proposals for using computers in an English or art classroom.

   Alternatively, if the course examines business communications, the tutor could establish a mythical company and the exercise can be constructed around that company's proposed purchase.

■ Exercise 5.2

Assessment interviews

Aims:

1. To enable students to practise interviewing skills;
2. To sensitize students to the difficulties of the interviewer;
3. To give students practice feedback on individual interview performance.

Equipment and materials required:
One room for the interviews and one for the remainder of the class, briefing sheets, video-recording and playback facilities.

Time required: (minimum two hours)
The exercise requires at least half an hour for briefing and preparation. Then interviews of about ten minutes should be held and recorded. Finally the recorded interviews should be played back to the whole class, requiring a period equivalent to the total length of the recordings.

Procedure:
Divide the class into groups of three or four. There should be an even number of groups. Half of the groups become interviewing groups and half become interviewee groups. Each group is given a copy of the appropriate briefing. Each interviewing group must then design an interview intended to assess the prospective candidate, while the interviewee groups select one of their members to be interviewed and establish the strategy of self-presentation to be used in the interview.

One member of the interviewee group is then interviewed by a complete interviewing group and the interview is recorded. When all interviews have been carried out the recordings are played back to the whole class and the performance of both interviewees and interviewers evaluated. The class can be asked to rank the performance of the groups and to select the best candidate. The students who appear on the recording should be asked to comment on their own performance, failings and good points.

Information for the students:

BRIEFING FOR INTERVIEWING GROUPS

> You are a management team for British Rail who require a young administrator to keep records and provide statistical information on the performance of a number of stations in your region, which

will involve liaising with a number of station personnel as well as the general public. You must decide on the interviewing strategy to adopt and the questions it is necessary to ask to discover the best candidate. Try to assess the degree of interest the candidate has in the job and in British Rail, his/her intelligence, technical level and personality. You must decide on the criteria that make up a good candidate and how to assess those criteria. Following the interview you must write a brief recommendation for your superiors.

BRIEFING FOR INTERVIEWEE GROUPS

You must select one of your members who will be interviewed for a placement with British Rail in an administrative post. The group must select the best candidate available and decide how he/she should present him/herself in the interview. Try to anticipate the kind of questions to be asked and suitable answers. Decide on good features of experience, expertise or personality that you wish to capitalize on and put forward. Try to identify weaknesses that could cause problems and decide how to handle questions in these areas. Think of one or two intelligent questions you can ask, given the opportunity.

Supporting information for the tutor:

Apart from the utilitarian value of recording the interview, cameras cause a degree of stress in the students, making the exercise a fair simulation of the real situation.

Either prior to the exercise or as part of the plenary session give a short lecture on the following:

WHAT INTERVIEWERS LOOK AT:

1. Physical make-up (capacity to cope with the physical demands of the job)
2. Attainment (qualifications and experience in relevant areas)
3. General intelligence (ability to respond quickly and ably and to cope with problems)
4. Special aptitudes (areas of particularly relevant experience or specialized knowledge)
5. Interests (indexes of personality, attitude and energy)
6. Disposition (personality, attitude to work and to this kind of work, ability to get on with people, to make decisions, to cope with pressure)
7. Circumstances (domestic or personal circumstances which may affect employment).

PROBLEMS WITH THE INTERVIEW

1. It makes people tense (but a little nervousness makes for a

good performance)

2. It favours good actors (so cultivate your self-image and self-presentation)
3. Different interviewers assess differently (so try to identify the interviewer most likely to view you favourably)
4. It has poor predictability (success in interviews only really correlates with success in interviews)
5. It creates a halo effect (if you start well allowances are made for later mistakes; if you start badly it might colour the whole of the rest of the interview).

Supporting bibliography and references:
Bergin, F J (1976) *Practical Communication.* Pitman.
Fisher, Cassie W and Constantine, T (1977) *Student's Guide to Success.* Macmillan.
Wise, A and Wise, N (1971) *Talking for Management.* Pitman.

Variations:

1. If video equipment is unavailable either use audio-recording equipment or arrange observers as in exercise 5.1. Each observer should have a separate responsibility, such as recording non-verbal communication or counting the number of closed questions.

2. If the class is small a useful variation is to use the same interviewing panel to interview all the remainder of the class and to produce a comparative assessment at the end of the session.

3. The roles can be reversed so that all students gain experience of both roles. Most interviewers in professional positions have no training.

4. If the above scenario is too remote from the likely jobs or placements of your students then vary it. However, try to ensure that all students will have at least some general knowledge of the organization and give the interviewers sufficient leeway to enable them to tailor the post to their own satisfaction and knowledge.

5. As part of a more extended simulation, interviewer groups can be asked to obtain or design a job specification. Interviewee groups then obtain that specification and construct a curriculum vitae for their chosen candidate which is returned to the interviewers prior to the interview.

6. *School variation*

Schools may be unable to use two rooms simultaneously, in which case the interviews must be conducted either in some 'protected' part of the normal classroom or at some time outside the normal curriculum. Alternatively, all interviews might be conducted simultaneously in a suitably divided room such as an assembly hall.

Related exercises: 2.4, 2.5 and Topic 4.

Exercise 5.3

The structure of selection interviews

Aims:

1. To introduce students to some of the problems of interviewing;
2. To guide the students through a 'structured approach' to interviewing.

Equipment and materials required:
Lecture materials, 'observer's notes', video recorder, camera and playback facilities. (Previously distributed — copies of job descriptions, together with application forms or details of curriculum vitaes (CVs) to be completed by all the class.)

Time required: (minimum two hours)
Approximately 20 minutes will be required for the introductory lecture, and a further 20 minutes for preparation by interview panels. Each interview simulation should run for about 15 minutes and require a further 20 minutes for playback and discussion.

Procedure:
Prior to running this exercise, all students should be asked to 'apply' for a specified job by completing application forms or writing CVs. The introductory lecture on 'the structure of a selection interview' can also be given in an earlier session, if wished.

In the interview simulation, the students play the roles of both interviewers and interviewees. Thus, the class should be divided into interview panels (two to four students in each) and one student in each panel designated as the interviewee for another panel.

The panels are asked to concentrate on the structure of their interview. Thus, each panel should spend the first five to ten minutes of its preparation time deciding this structure and allocating roles for the interview. After this time, each panel should be given the application form or CV of its candidate, and asked to continue preparation.

Each panel then conducts its interview in turn, while other members of the class write 'observer's notes'. Each interview is video-recorded, and discussed on replay (it is probably better to record two or three interviews and then replay and discuss).

Information for the students:
The students will obviously require a lecture on the structure of selection interviews prior to the commencement of the exercise.

For the simulation, students should be asked to 'be themselves' wherever possible. However, they should also regard any information given by the interviewee as 'true only in the context of the simulation'.

The students should be given the following 'observer's notes' to use while they are watching the interviews.

For each of the following, how did the interviewers:

IN OPENING THE INTERVIEW

1. Establish their identity?
2. Explain the purpose?
3. Outline the structure?
4. Establish rapport?

IN CONDUCTING THE INTERVIEW

5. Divide the interview into sections?
6. Sequence the sections?
7. Signpost the sections?

IN CLOSING THE INTERVIEW

8. Give the candidate an opportunity to ask questions?
9. Outline next steps?
10. Thank the interviewee?

Supporting information for the tutor:
Some of the problems with selection interviews are:

— they make people tense;
— they favour good actors;

— interviewers differ in their assessments;
— the 'halo' effect colours interviewers' judgements.

One way of tackling these problems is to adopt a 'structured approach' in the interview, and in the assessment of the interviewees. Thus, the interview overall should be seen as falling into three parts: an opening, the main part, and a closing. Each part of the interview has its own functions, style and structure.

The opening should establish the identity of the participants and the purpose of the interview. But it is also very important at this stage to put the interviewee at ease.

In preparing for the main part of a selection interview, one needs to ask three questions:

1. What does the job require?
2. What do you know about the candidate?
3. What do you need to know?

Clearly, the answers to (1) and (2) are to be found in the job description and the application form (or CV) respectively. Comparison of these answers enables one to answer (3), which will then provide the basis for the main 'information getting' part of the interview.

This 'information getting' is all the more effective if one uses a set of 'key areas' consistently for each candidate. Thus, one might have as key areas: education and qualifications; experience; motivation; interpersonal skills; etc. These areas can then provide the structure for this main part of the interview, with each interviewer taking responsibility for one or two areas.

The closing stage of the interview normally commences by asking the interviewee if he/she has any questions to ask. (A useful addition to this is to ask if the candidate has any information which he/she wishes to draw to the attention of the panel.) The interviewee should also be told how and when he or she can expect to hear the outcome of the interview and, finally, thanked for attending. Throughout the closing sequence, the emphasis should be on reinforcing (or repairing) the relationship established.

LECTURE NOTES ON THE STRUCTURE OF A SELECTION INTERVIEW

1. *Opening the interview*
   Establish identity

Explain purpose
Outline structure
Establish rapport

2. *The main stage in the interview*
Remember to *section*, *sequence* and *signpost*.
Use key areas to develop a system plan for the interview, eg:
Education (institutions; qualifications)
Work experience (training; relevant experience; other)
Motivation (Why this work? What qualities can the candidate offer?)
Interpersonal competence (ability to relate to others, withstand pressure, work as a team member)
Circumstances (accommodation, travelling, age, likely to stay?)

3. *Closing the interview*
Ask candidate for questions
Reinforce/repair relationship
Outline next steps
Thank interviewee.

Supporting bibliography and references:
Stanton, N (1982) *The Business of Communicating.* Pan.

Variations:

1. Use audiotape recording to give feedback.

2. Where no recording facilities are available, use only the 'observer's notes' for feedback.

3. Only allow one-third of the class to conduct their interviews in this exercise. Then allow one-third for 'interviewer skills' exercise, and the remaining third for 'interviewee skills' exercise.

Related exercises: 2.4, 2.5 and Topic 4.

■ **Exercise 5.4**

Interviewer skills in selection interviews

Aims:

1. To introduce students to some of the problems of interviewing;

2. To give the students practice in the skills required by interviewers.

Equipment and materials required:
Lecture materials, 'observer's notes', video recorder, camera and playback facilities. (Previously distributed — copies of job descriptions, together with application forms or details of curriculum vitaes (CVs) to be completed by all the class.)

Time required: (minimum two hours)
Approximately 20 minutes will be required for the introductory lecture, and a further 20 minutes for preparation by interview panels. Each interview simulation should run for about 15 minutes and require a further 20 minutes for playback and discussion.

Procedure:
Prior to running this exercise, all students should be asked to 'apply' for a specified job by completing application forms or writing CVs. The introductory lecture on 'the skills of interviewing' can also be given in an earlier session, if wished. In the interview simulation, the students play the roles of both interviewers and interviewees. Thus, the class should be divided into interview panels (two to four students in each) and one student in each panel designated as the interviewee for another panel.

The panels are asked to concentrate on the use of 'interviewer skills' in the interview. Thus, each panel should spend its preparation time devising suitable questions and follow-ups.

Each panel then conducts its interview in turn, while other members of the class write 'observer's notes'. Each interview is video-recorded, and discussed on replay (it is probably better to record two or three interviews and then replay and discuss).

Information for the students:
The students will require a lecture on the skills required by interviewers, prior to the commencement of the exercise. (It would also be advisable to give the students practice in listening and questioning skills, using the exercises given in this book.)

For the simulation, students should be asked to 'be themselves' wherever possible. However, they should also regard any information given by the interviewee as 'true only in the context of the simulation'.

The students should be given the following 'observer's notes' to use while they are watching the interviews:

97

OBSERVER'S NOTES

For each of the following, how did the interviewers perform?
(Give examples wherever possible):

In establishing rapport?
Methods used?
How successful?

If used, were the following question types used appropriately?
(Give examples)
   1. Closed questions
   2. Multiple-choice type
   3. Identification type
   4. Open-ended questions

Were any problematic question forms used?
(Give examples)
   5. Leading questions
   6. Multiple questions
   7. Non-questions

Were follow-ups used?
(Give examples)
   8. Simple prompt
   9. Silence
  10. Key-word mirroring
  11. Reflection: of ideas, of feelings
  12. Probe questions.

Supporting information for the tutor:
In the opening stage of a selection interview it is important to establish a rapport with the interviewee. The interviewers should show themselves to be courteous, warm and sincere. The interviewee should be made to feel at ease and respected. This rapport can be established in this opening stage by using small talk, and extending simple courtesies to the interviewee.

   Interviewers need to be aware of the two basic kinds of questions, viz. closed and open questions. The former are those to which there are really only one- or two-word answers. The latter, on the other hand, are 'open' in the sense that the interviewee is required to answer at greater length, although the exact length is determined by him/her. Clearly, in selection interviewing, the interviewers should really be using 'open' questions much of the time.

   Inexperienced interviewers have a tendency to ask questions

which have one of the following problematic forms:

1. Leading questions — these give the interviewee the answer that is required, eg 'This job requires you to work with people. Are you good at working with people?';
2. Multiple questions — several questions in one;
3. Non-questions — these are really statements by the interviewer, and all the interviewee has to do is to agree.

Having asked a suitable question and got the interviewee talking, the interviewer then needs to be able to keep him/her talking so as to obtain the required information on that topic. This means being able to follow-up with questions or other prompts. To encourage someone to continue talking, it is often sufficient simply to remain silent, or to say 'yes' or 'mmm' in a suitable tone. If you wish the interviewee to talk more about a particular aspect of his/her answer, then simply saying one or two 'key' words in a questioning tone will usually be sufficient.

To ensure that the interviewee carries on talking about the desired topic, the interviewer can ask a 'probe' question. These questions probe for:

— Reasons ('Why did you do . . .?')
— Examples ('Can you give me an example of that?')
— Justification ('Why do you think that . . .?')
— Clarification ('Would you explain?')
— Elaboration ('Tell me more about . . .?').

LECTURE NOTES ON THE SKILLS OF A SELECTION INTERVIEWER

1. *Establishing rapport*
   Personality — courtesy, warmth, sincerity.
   Demonstrate respect — interest, attention, agreement.
   Extraneous conversation — small talk, common ground.
   Simple courtesies — thanks, comfort, explanation.

2. *Questioning*
   Closed questions
   (a) Yes-no type: 'Have you read the job description?'
   (b) Multiple-choice type: 'Were you with your last firm for more or less than six months?'
   (c) Identification type: 'Which was your best subject?'
   Open-ended questions
   (a) 'Tell me about your work.'
   (b) 'What do you think about this problem?'

3. *Problematic question forms*
   Leading questions
   Multiple questions
   Non-questions

4. *Follow-ups*
   Simple prompt — 'Yes', 'Go on'
   Silence
   Key-word mirroring
   Probe questions — 'Why do you think that?'

Supporting bibliography and references:
Hargie, O, Saunders, C and Dickson, D (1981) *Social Skills in Interpersonal Communication.* Croom Helm.
Stanton, N (1982) *The Business of Communicating.* Pan.

Variations:

1. Use audiotape recording to give feedback.

2. Where no recording facilities are available, use only 'observer's notes' for feedback.

3. Allow one-third of the class to conduct their interviews in the 'interview structure' exercise, then allow one-third for this exercise, and the remaining third for 'interviewee skills' exercise.

Related exercises: 2.4, 2.5 and Topic 4.

■ Exercise 5.5

Thinking about being interviewed

Aims:

1. To encourage students to think about some of the problems of being interviewed;
2. To enable the students to share ideas and fears about being interviewed;
3. To encourage students to devise suitable strategies to overcome the problems and fears of being interviewed;
4. To give the students a checklist of actions to be taken in preparing for an interview.

Equipment and materials required:
Overhead projector, OHP transparencies and pens (sufficient for number of students in class divided by four). Alternatively, a

flipchart and felt pens may be used, depending on the class size and location.

Time required:
Approximately 45 minutes.

Procedure:
In stage 1 of this exercise, the class is divided into pairs and each pair asked to produce a list of things that they should do in order to prepare for being interviewed. After about 10 minutes, each pair should be joined with one other, and the resulting group of four asked to create a set of guidelines on 'Preparing for, and being interviewed' (see below for a more detailed specification of the brief). About 20 minutes should be allowed for this stage.

In the final stage of the exercise, each group presents its set of guidelines to the rest of the class. Allow a couple of minutes per presentation. If the class is a very large one, it may be advisable to select five or six groups to present their guidelines.

Information for the students:
The students should be given the following brief:

STAGE 1 — In pairs (10 minutes):

(a) What should you do to prepare for being interviewed?

STAGE 2 — In fours (20 minutes):

(b) Share the lists obtained in Stage 1 and generate new ideas.
(c) Generate ideas on how an interviewee can improve his/her performance during an interview (eg what to do about nerves).
(d) From (b) and (c), create a set of guidelines on 'Preparing for, and being interviewed'.
(e) List your guidelines on the OHP transparency provided.
(f) Appoint someone to present your group's ideas to the rest of the class.

STAGE 3 — Whole class (15 minutes):

(g) Present ideas and discuss.

Supporting information for the tutor:
During the presentation and discussion of the guidelines for 'Preparing for and being interviewed', the following are some of the points that you should seek to elicit:

1. PREPARATION

The job: re-read literature, review your knowledge of the work.
Your application: re-read it, check for likely questions.
Questions you might be asked: prepare your answers.
Questions you wish to ask: make a note of these (on a small card!).

2. NON-VERBAL BEHAVIOUR DURING THE INTERVIEW

Appearance: be clean, tidy, attractive.
Posture: attentive, ready for action, not slouched.
Nerves: channel energy into gestures of emphasis.
Voice: modulate to emphasize and show interest.
Demonstrate respect: show interest, do not smoke or argue.

3. ANSWERING IN THE INTERVIEW

Think: take time to think before replying.
Clarify: if unsure of question, restate or ask.
Language: speak normally, do not try to use 'formal language'.
Length: gauge length of answer required.
Exemplify: give examples to support what you are saying.

Supporting bibliography and references:
Bufton, I, Aram, J and Roberts, L (1983) *Applications and Interviews.* AGCAS Careers Information Booklet. Central Services Unit for University and Polytechnic Careers and Appointments Services (CSU).
Stanton, N (1982) *The Business of Communicating.* Pan.

Variations:

1. Combine the pairs to form larger groups (six or eight students) in stage 2.

2. Combine the groups of four to form groups of eight in stage 2(d).

Related exercises: 1.2, 2.4, 2.5 and Topic 4.

Exercise 5.6

Interviewee skills in selection interviews

Aims:

1. To introduce students to some of the problems of being interviewed;
2. To give the students practice in the skills of being interviewed.

Equipment and materials required:
Lecture materials, 'observer's notes', video recorder, camera and playback facilities. (Previously distributed – copies of job descriptions, together with application forms or details of curriculum vitaes (CVs) to be completed by all the class.)

Time required: (minimum two hours)
Approximately 15 minutes will be required for the introductory lecture/discussion, and a further 20 minutes for preparation by interview panels. Each interview simulation should run for about 15 minutes and require a further 20 minutes for playback and discussion.

Procedure:
Prior to running this exercise, all students should be asked to 'apply' for a specified job by completing application forms or writing CVs. The introductory lecture on 'the skills of being interviewed' can also be given in an earlier session, if wished.

In the interview simulation, the students play the roles of both interviewers and interviewees. Thus, the class should be divided into interview panels (two to four students in each) and one student in each panel designated as the interviewee for another panel.

Each panel should spend its preparation time planning the structure of its interview and devising suitable questions and follow-ups.

Each panel then conducts its interview in turn, while other members of the class write 'observer's notes' on the performance of the interviewee. Each interview is video-recorded, and discussed on replay (it is probably better to record two or three interviews and then replay and discuss).

Information for the students:
The students will require a lecture/discussion on the skills required by interviewees, prior to the commencement of the exercise.

For the simulation, students should be asked to 'be themselves' wherever possible. However, they should also regard any information given by the interviewee as 'true only in the context of the simulation'.

The students should be given the following 'observer's notes' to use while they are watching the interviews:

For each of the following, how did the interviewee perform?
(Examples of the sort of comment required are given in brackets.)

1. *Posture* (eg slouched, attentive, relaxed)
2. *Voice quality* (eg 'used to motivate', 'show interest', 'uninteresting')
3. *Voice level* (eg 'too quiet', 'too loud', 'mumbled', 'just right')
4. *Non-verbal signals* (eg 'distracting', 'emphasizing', 'showing enthusiasm')
5. *Length of answers* (eg 'appropriate', 'too short', 'too long')
6. *Quality of answering* (eg 'clear', 'to the point', 'thought out')
7. *Appropriateness of answers* (give examples of good answers and examples of those to be improved by the interviewee)
8. *Examples/illustrations* given to support answers (eg 'answers general and unsupported', 'answers well-supported')
9. *Knowledge* (eg 'authoritative', 'did not know enough')
10. *Maintenance of interest* (eg 'held my interest', 'my attention wandered').

The interviewers can be given the following assessment schedule:

INTERVIEW ASSESSMENT

Rating — circle appropriate number using the following key:

5 outstanding; 4 suitable; 3 possible; 2 doubtful; 1 unsuitable. (Give examples to justify assessment wherever possible):

1. *Impact on interviewer*
   (Appearance, speech, manner.)

| 5 | 4 | 3 | 2 | 1 |

2. *Intelligence*
   (Achievement, judgement, insight.)

   | 5 | 4 | 3 | 2 | 1 |

3. *Experience*
   (Training, work experience.)

   | 5 | 4 | 3 | 2 | 1 |

4. *Interpersonal competence*
   (Ability to relate to others.)

   | 5 | 4 | 3 | 2 | 1 |

5. *Motivation*
   (Why this job? Ambitions, drive.)

   | 5 | 4 | 3 | 2 | 1 |

Supporting information for the tutor:
Most students know the sort of things that they should do in order to prepare for an interview. Thus, the lecture should aim at giving them a checklist so as to encourage them actually to act in accordance with what they know. Similarly, students usually have some good ideas about how they should 'behave' in interviews. Again, the lecture can be largely seen as providing a checklist. (See the lecture notes below for further details.)

In the discussion after the simulations, it is very important to protect the self-esteem of the interviewees and generally to make them feel more confident. Thus, the emphasis should be on finding good points for each interviewee. Those points which are noted as requiring improvement should only be commented upon if it is actually possible for the interviewee to improve them (and such points should be balanced by an equal number of good points). For each simulated interview, restrict comments to a few major items.

LECTURE NOTES ON BEING INTERVIEWED

1. *Preparation*
   The job: re-read literature, review your knowledge of the work.
   Your application: re-read it, check for likely questions.
   Questions you might be asked: prepare your answers.
   Questions you wish to ask: make a note of these (on a small card!).

105

2. *Non-verbal behaviour*
   Appearance: be clean, tidy, attractive.
   Posture: attentive, ready for action, not slouched.
   Nerves: channel energy into gestures of emphasis.
   Voice: modulate to emphasize and show interest.
   Demonstrate respect: show interest, do not smoke or argue.

3. *Answering*
   Think: take time to think before replying.
   Clarify: if unsure of question, restate or ask.
   Language: speak normally, do not try to use 'formal language'.
   Length: gauge length of answer required.
   Exemplify: give examples to support what you are saying.

Supporting bibliography and references:
Bufton, I, Aram, J and Roberts, L (1983) *Applications and Interviews*. AGCAS Careers Information Booklet. Central Services Unit for University and Polytechnic Careers and Appointments Services (CSU).
Stanton, N (1982) *The Business of Communicating*. Pan.

Variations:

1. Use audiotape recording to give feedback.

2. Where no recording facilities are available, use only 'observer's notes' and 'interviewer's assessments' for feedback.

3. Allow one-third of the class to conduct their interviews in the 'interview structure' exercise, one-third in the 'interviewer skills' exercise, and the remaining third in this exercise.

4. Instead of giving a lecture on being interviewed, use exercise 5.5.

5. *School variation*
   If it is inappropriate to use employment interviews and CVs some other personal assessment scenario should be used. It may be sufficient to consider part-time and vacation employment or selection interviews for a place in higher education. As part of an extended project on business structures and communication, selection interviews can be simulated or, if the course deals with the media, then the interview could be for a post in journalism or broadcasting.
   Alternatively pupils may be more highly motivated by interviews for positions of responsibility or competition

within the school, such as school committees, teams or organizations. Even if no such interview is carried out in reality, the interview can be presented as a means of structuring and appraising a pupil's abilities, experience and confidence.

Related exercises: 2.4, 2.5 and Topic 4.

Exercise 5.7

Self-motivation

Aims:

1. To encourage students to evaluate their own motivations;
2. To provide students with a practical basis upon which to begin a real employment interview.

Equipment and materials required:
A copy of the self-evaluation sheet for each student.

Time required: (minimum 20 minutes)
Approximately five minutes will be required for the briefing. Allow about 15 minutes for students to carry out their evaluations. As the aim of the exercise is to provide students with a basis for a real interview it can be carried out in their own time if desired.

Procedure:
Give each student a copy of the self-evaluation sheet and ask them to rate themselves honestly.

Information for the students:

The form below is intended to provide you with self-evaluation on your motivation for work. Assess yourself honestly and you will have a practical basis on which to build an interview or curriculum vitae. It should also help you decide on the kind of work you would prefer. For each of the possible characteristics of a job listed below, indicate the strength of motivation it would give you, with 5 being high and 1 low. When you have finished you should be able to identify the kind of job that you would find most attractive. When you come to investigate jobs that you wish to apply for, use the same form to evaluate the job, rating it on the degree to which each of those features is offered. This will give you some indication of the degree of correspondence between your desires and the actual characteristics of the job.

EVALUATION OF MOTIVATION

	1	2	3	4	5
1. Job security					
2. Meeting other people					
3. Easy work					
4. Demanding work					
5. Good salary					
6. Attractive location					
7. Helps other people					
8. Uses existing skill					
9. Learning new skills					
10. High responsibility					
11. Good promotion prospects					
12. Long vacations					
13. Travel opportunities					
14. Prestigious occupation					
15. Flexitime					
16. Highly structured routine					
17. Intellectually stimulating					
18. Good social contacts					
19. Significant decision making					
20. Good rewards for good work					

Supporting information for the tutor:
Little preamble or discussion is needed other than to stress the need for self-knowledge in applying for, obtaining and enjoying employment. Motivation is the single most important factor in job satisfaction and a characteristic that most interviewers attempt to assess. If a student understands his/her own motivation he/she will be more able to convince prospective employers. If a student identifies weaknesses then these may be rectifiable. You may wish to use the results of the evaluation as the basis of a class on improving self-motivation or for private career tutorials with individual students.

Supporting bibliography and references:
Fisher, Cassie W and Constantine, T (1977) *Student's Guide to Success.* Macmillan.

Variations:

1. The same form can be used to evaluate various jobs that students think they may enjoy to assess the degree of correspondence between the job and the student's requirements. This can be done by obtaining application forms and job specifications for real advertised posts and asking the students to carry out the exercise.

2. *School variation*
   Similar exercises can be run to help pupils decide on the subjects they wish to pursue in following years at school or in higher education. In these cases some of the motivating factors will differ from the sheet given so the tutor may need to prepare a different sheet (altering, for example, numbers 1, 2, 5, 6, 11, 12, 13, 15, 18, 19).

   However, a better strategy is to construct a preliminary exercise in which the pupils themselves prepare an evaluation sheet appropriate to the task. This encourages students to think about motivation and their own decisions in two stages:
   1. Considering the factors that might affect motivation in general and in respect of a particular set of subject areas;
   2. Considering their own personal motivations in the light of factors they have determined as significant.

   It is important that the pupils do not know about the intended second stage before they carry out the first stage. If they are aware of the purpose of their Evaluation of Motivation sheets they will construct them in the light of their own particular preferences. Ensure also that all the pupil-designed motivation schemes can benefit from the thoughts of the whole class, by holding a plenary session, by attempting a universal summary of all factors thought important or by arranging for each designing pupil group to report back before any finalize their sheets.

Topic 6: Group communication

■ Exercise 6.1

Introduction to group work

Aims:

1. To introduce students to working in groups;
2. To encourage students to think about some of the problems of working in groups;
3. To enable the students to share ideas about working in groups;
4. To encourage students to devise suitable strategies to overcome the problems of working in groups;
5. To introduce the topic of alternative energy.

Equipment and materials required:
No equipment is necessary, though the following can be used if wished: overhead projector, OHP transparencies and pens (sufficient for number of students in class divided by six).

Time required:
Approximately 60 minutes.

Procedure:
In stage 1 of this exercise, the class is divided into pairs and each pair asked to produce a list of alternative sources of energy. After about five minutes, each pair should be joined with two others, and the resulting group of six asked to create a combined list of sources, and to evaluate them (see below for a more detailed specification of the brief). About 20 minutes should be allowed for this stage.

In the next stage of the exercise, each group presents its findings to the rest of the class. Allow about 15 minutes for the presentations and discussion. (If the class is a very large one, it may be advisable to select just a few groups to present their findings.)

In stage 4, each student is given a checklist to use to evaluate the group's performance. After a few minutes, the students in each group share their ideas and produce an agreed group evaluation. The exercise finishes with a class discussion about working in groups, using the group evaluations as a basis for discussion.

Information for the students:
The students should be given the following brief:

STAGE 1 — In pairs (5 minutes):

Discuss and write down a list of alternative sources of energy.

STAGE 2 — In groups (20 minutes):

(a) Share the lists obtained in stage 1, generate new ideas, and produce an agreed list for the group.
(b) Of each source state if it is suitable for generating electricity or whether it is more suitable for use in some other way.
(c) On which sources, if any, should the Department of Energy encourage research and development by large-scale funding?
(d) Appoint someone to present your group's ideas to the rest of the class.

STAGE 3 — Whole class (15 minutes):

Present ideas and discuss.

STAGE 4 — Individually (3 minutes):

Evaluate your group's performance.

STAGE 5 — In groups (5 minutes):

(a) Share evaluations.
(b) Produce an agreed evaluation for the whole group.

STAGE 6 — Whole class (12 minutes):

Present ideas and discuss.

The following can be used as a checklist for stage 4:

GROUP EVALUATION CHECKLIST

1. For your group, please rate on a scale of 1 to 5 (low to high) the extent to which:
   (a) everybody participated
   (b) members listened to each other
   (c) members supported and helped each other
   (d) quiet members were encouraged to talk
2. What can the members of your group be pleased about in the way they worked together?
3. If your group were to repeat the exercise, is there anything the group could change to improve the way the members worked together?

Supporting information for the tutor:
Clearly, there are two 'learning aspects' to this 'introductory' exercise, viz. working in groups and alternative energy. In each case the main aims are to introduce students to the topic and

raise awareness about it, rather than inculcate specific ideas.

With regard to the topic of working in groups, the following are some of the points that you should seek to elicit during the class discussion.

To work effectively, the group should consider:

1. Adopting a strategy to encourage everyone to participate;
2. How to prevent individuals dominating the discussion;
3. Electing a leader to chair the discussion;
4. Appointing one person to be responsible for writing down ideas on a large sheet of paper for all the group to see;
5. How to deal with conflicts.

Supporting bibliography and references:
Appel, A L (1984) *A Practical Approach to Human Behaviour in Business.* Charles E Merrill.

Variations:

The topic for group work is unimportant. We have used alternative energy as one topic in several exercises throughout this book to enable construction of a course using different communication skills with one 'technical' content area.

However, any topic with the following characteristics can be used and can replace alternative energy in all exercises that use it.

(a) It has multiple aspects, eg it involves economic, social, political, technical, media and organizational issues.
(b) It can be subdivided into several subtopics so that different groups or individuals can work on these.
(c) It is connected with some other work the students are currently engaged in. For example, science students may be motivated by computing; pupils studying O or A levels may be interested in assessment systems; all students may carry out projects on ways of presenting information.

Related exercises: 1.1 and 3.5.

■ Exercise 6.2

Group organization

Aims:

1. To give students practice in elementary problem solving and group communication;

2. To demonstrate that communicative differences can depend on group organization;
3. To encourage students to evaluate groups in which they participate.

Equipment and materials required:
A large room suitable for several small groups. It is important that seating can be arranged to suit the group structure of each group.

Time required: (minimum 20 minutes)
The exercise requires five minutes' briefing, at least 20 minutes for the group discussion and 10 to 15 minutes' plenary discussion.

Procedure:
Prior to the class, arbitrarily identify groups of unequal size. Where other obvious variables exist in the class, such as race, social class, sex or educational background, try to keep the groups as random as possible. Arrange the seating and divide the class into groups which conform to the following structures:

1. Seated in a horseshoe
2. Seated in a circle
3. Seated in a straight line
4. Seated in two rows facing each other across a desk
5. Has only three members
6. Has more than six members
7. One chair faces the rest. This is the chairperson of this group and he/she must regulate all conversation in the group.

Each group must be given a different protocol for communicating and must stick to it throughout the discussion. These should include:

1. Members can only speak when the chairperson gives them permission and must stop when told.
2. Anyone can speak at any time.
3. Members of the group can only speak to people sitting next to them.
4. People can only speak if previously spoken to (ie in response to a question or command from someone else).
5. Members must speak strictly in turn. (This can be established as alphabetical order of names or clockwise by seating.)

Because classes differ in size, tutors should decide on the most appropriate structures and protocols for a given class. We

113

recommend that at least four groups be formed, and each given a different structure and protocol.

Once groups have been arranged and briefed they should be given 20 minutes to discover the feature common to all members of the group. A record should be kept of the order in which groups complete the task.

Information for the students:

Briefing:

> Each group has been set up with a particular seating arrangement and a particular communication protocol. These must be rigidly adhered to throughout the exercise.
>
> The tutor has looked at the records of each student and all members of each group have been selected because they have something in common. The group must discover what this common characteristic is within the 20 minutes available.

Supporting information for the tutor:

The exercise is designed so that random groups of individuals must find a common characteristic which is not predetermined. As the tutor has not decided on these features beforehand he/she must accept whatever decision seems to satisfy the group. Those variables which affect success in achieving the task will primarily be the communicative abilities of the members of the groups and the organization of each group. Tutors should select group structures and protocols (from the 35 possible) which are most suitable to the size and nature of the class.

Large groups should find the task harder than small groups. Linear groups will find it harder than circular groups. Groups arranged in confrontation may have more debate. The more restricted the permitted channel of communication the fewer the number of communications and the less valuable will be the average contribution. However, groups which allow complete freedom of communication, especially if large, will create more noise and confusion in their discussion and may split into subgroups.

The most successful group in this task is likely to be a small group (three to four members) arranged in a circle and administered by a nominal chairperson. The least successful will be a large group linearly arranged with a highly restricted channel of communication.

These points should emerge from the discussion when 20 minutes have elapsed. If several groups have succeeded in finding common features, examine the time taken to achieve this. Ask the class to explain why some groups were more successful than others. If few groups succeed in the available time ask each group in turn for an evaluation of the ease/difficulty of the task and ask them to explain why those diffculties arose.

The exercise can be generalized to any situation in which more than two people are occupied on the same task. The same communicative structures can be found not only in meetings, such as committee meetings, but in situations where the communication is through telephone, memorandum or letter, eg where an administrative hierarchy constrains channels of communication.

Supporting bibliography and references:
Dineen, J (1977) *Talking Your Way to Success.* Thorsons.
Fisher, Cassie W and Constantine, T (1977) *Student's Guide to Success.* Macmillan.
Goodworth, C T (1980) *Effective Speaking and Presentation for the Company Executive.* Hutchinson.
Maude, B (1974) *Practical Communication for Managers.* Longman.

Variations:

1. The exercise can be combined with other group problem-solving exercises if time is short, so that several aspects of group structure and success can be discussed simultaneously.

2. If the class is small a useful variation is to use only two types of group, groups of four in circles and groups of six or more in a row with a restrictive protocol. More groups of the first kind should finish before groups of the second.

Exercise 6.3

Decision making

Aims:

1. To introduce students to some of the problems of group decision making;
2. To compare the results of individual and group decision making;
3. To encourage students to devise suitable strategies to overcome the problems of group decision making.

Equipment and materials required:
Copies of the Individual Worksheets and Group Record Forms (sufficient for all the students in the class) and several calculators.

Time required:
Approximately one hour.

Procedure:
In stage 1 of this exercise, each person in the class is asked to complete the task specified on the Individual Worksheet. The task is to rank a list of ten items in the same order as that produced by a Market & Opinion Research International (MORI) survey. The class is then divided into groups of about five or six members. Each person is then supplied with a Group Record Form, and each group asked to reach a decision about the task. About 20 minutes should be allowed for this stage.

As each group finishes the task, each member is given a checklist (see the Group Evaluation Checklist in exercise 6.1) to use to evaluate the group's performance. After a few minutes, the students in the group share their ideas and produce an agreed group evaluation.

When all the groups have finished, the class is given the MORI ranking. The students then calculate the individual and group error scores by comparing their rankings with the MORI ranking.

The exercise finishes with a class discussion about working in groups, using the scores and the group evaluations as a basis for discussion.

Information for the students:
In stage 1, the students should be given the following Individual Worksheet:

A MINIMUM STANDARD OF LIVING

In 1983 London Weekend Television commissioned Market & Opinion Research International (MORI) to survey 1174 people in Britain as to what they thought constituted an unacceptably low standard of living.

The following ten items were described as necessary for a minimum standard of living by more than 50 per cent of the survey sample. Your task is to rank these items in the same order of necessity as established by the survey.

Place the number 1 by the item you believe most people would consider necessary, number 2 by the second most necessary, and so on through to number 10.

— Public transport for one's needs
— Carpets in living rooms and bedrooms
— Leisure equipment for children, eg bicycle
— Heating to warm living areas of the home
— Washing machine
— Three meals a day for children
— Television
— Bath (not shared with another household)
— Self-contained accommodation
— Meat or fish every other day

In stage 2, each student should be given the following Group Record Form on which to record the rankings of his/her fellow group members (in columns A to F). Each group is then told to complete the task again and so arrive at a group decision which is then recorded in column G.

	LISTS OF RANKINGS							
	by Members						by Group	by MORI
	A	B	C	D	E	F	G	M
Public transport								
Carpets								
Leisure equipment								
Heating								
Washing machine								
Three meals a day								
Television								
Bath								
Accommodation								
Daily meat or fish								
ERROR SCORES								

Supporting information for the tutor:
According to the MORI survey, the 'ranking by necessity' of the ten items was as follows:

3   Public transport for one's needs
6   Carpets in living rooms and bedrooms
9   Leisure equipment for children, eg bicycle
1   Heating to warm living areas of the home
7   Washing machine
4   Three meals a day for children
10 Television
2   Bath (not shared with another household)
5   Self-contained accommodation
8   Meat or fish every other day

After the students have been given the above list, they can calculate how well they and their group have performed. To calculate the error score for an individual student:

1. For each item on the list compute the difference between the student's ranking and the MORI ranking;
2. Square the differences (this penalizes large errors);
3. Add the squares up.

The same procedure can then be used to calculate the group error score.

Using these scores together with the other information collected on the Group Record Forms, a variety of observations can be made:

1. *Adequacy of decision making* — this can be assessed in terms of the total error scores.
2. *Group synergy* — this is measured by the extent to which the group error score is less than that of the most proficient member.
3. *Utilization of resources* — by comparing the group, MORI and members' rankings for a particular item, it is possible to determine whether or not the best answer was utilized for that item.
4. *Creativity* — similarly, by comparing the group, MORI and members' rankings for a particular item, it is possible to determine whether or not the group 'created' a better answer than was previously available for that item.

It is useful to structure the debriefing discussion around the question of how the groups might improve their performance as measured by the above criteria. The following are some of the points that you should seek to elicit during this class discussion. To make effective decisions, the group members should:

1. Adopt a strategy to encourage everyone to participate and so maximize the utilization of resources;
2. Prevent individuals dominating the discussion;
3. Consider electing a leader to chair the discussion, if and when appropriate;
4. Deal with conflicts by discussion;
5. View differences in opinion as natural and helpful to the creative processes involved in decision making;
6. Remember that it is more important that the group should make an effective decision than that their own opinions be adopted.

Supporting bibliography and references:
Appell, A L (1984) *A Practical Approach to Human Behaviour in Business.* Charles E Merrill.
Hall, J and Watson, W H (1970) The effects of normative intervention on group decision-making performance. *Human Relations*, 23(4), pp.299-317.

Variation:

Use the 'NASA Moon Survival Problem' (Hall and Watson, 1970) as the group task.

Exercise 6.4

Group decision making

Aims:

1. To give students practice in group decision making;
2. To illustrate some of the problems of group decision making;
3. To encourage students to use logical and lateral thinking in problem solving.

Equipment and materials required:
Facilities for small group discussion and one set of five application forms and information sheets for each group.

Time required: (minimum 40 minutes)
Only two minutes will be required for the briefing. Allow about 30 minutes for making the decisions and a further ten minutes for comparison and discussion of the results.

Procedure:
Arrange the students in groups of five. Describe the task to the class, and then each group should be given a set of application forms and information sheets. As the information sheets differ, but are intended to appear the same, give each sheet to an individual student so no student has the opportunity initially to compare sheets. Keep a record on the blackboard of the time taken for each group to come to a decision and a record of the candidate selected in each case. When an incorrect decision is made record it but tell the group to try again. When all groups have reached a decision or time has expired hold a discussion on the difficulties of problem solving in groups.

Information for the students:

INFORMATION SHEET

You are a member of the appointments committee for the Department of Mathematics and Computing at Hardhit Polytechnic. The committee has to appoint a new lecturer. The candidate must have three science A levels and a science degree and must have good teaching experience, research experience and administrative experience. Candidates should be young (ie under 40). You have interviewed several candidates and have selected the candidate below as the best of your interviewees. The committee now has to choose which of the five different candidates is the most suitable for the job.

[*Note:* To be a member of the Institute of Applied Numbers you must have a science degree.]

Applicant: Mr Abercrombie
Age: 36
Nationality: British
A levels: Mathematics, Physics, English, French, Chemistry
Qualifications: BSc in Notional Computation
    Member of the Institute of Applied Numbers
    Member of the Society of Countable Sciences
Experience: 16 years' teaching at Bosworth Field
    Polytechnic
    10 years' experience of office work in teaching
Publications: How to Count without Fingers, *Journal of Numbers, Science and Complicated Theories*, June 1979.

INFORMATION SHEET

You are a member of the appointments committee for the Department of Mathematics and Computing at Hardhit Polytechnic. The committee has to appoint a new lecturer. The candidate must have three science A levels and a science degree and must have good teaching experience, research experience and administrative experience. Candidates should be young and should have the Certificate of Integerology.

    You have interviewed several candidates and have selected the candidate below as the best of your interviewees. The committee now has to choose which of the five different candidates is the most suitable for the job.

[*Note:* A science degree is signified by BSc. Anyone who has five or more years' teaching in a university is automatically awarded the Certificate of Integerology.]

Applicant: Miss Bastaple
Age: 38
Nationality: Australian
A levels: Physics, Computing, Chemistry
Qualifications: Member of the Institute of Applied Numbers
Certificate of Integerology (1979)
Experience: 14 years' teaching at Oregano University
12 years' experience as department head with many administrative responsibilities
Research Assistant to the National Project on Numerate Machines
Publications: Making Computers Count, *Journal of Numbers, Science and Complicated Theories*, July 1980
Time Series and Temporal Series, *Computing Science*, Dec 1980
Fundamentals of Set Theory, 1981
New Ideas in Mathematics, 1982.

INFORMATION SHEET

You are a member of the appointments committee for the Department of Mathematics and Computing at Hardhit Polytechnic. The committee has to appoint a new lecturer. The candidate must have three science A levels and a science degree and must have good teaching experience, research experience and administrative experience. Candidates should be young and a full member of the Institute of Applied Numbers.

You have interviewed several candidates and have selected the candidate below as the best of your interviewees. The committee now has to choose which of the five different candidates is the most suitable for the job.

[*Note:* As far as the Department is concerned Biology is not a science A level.]

Applicant: Mrs Claus
Age: 33
Nationality: Icelandic
A levels: Mathematics, Physics, Chemistry
Qualifications: Member of the Institute of Applied Numbers
Certificate of Integerology (1976)

Experience: 6 years' teaching at Winterfield Polytechnic,
5 years at Brougham University
Editor of the *Journal of Numbers* (1977-1982)
Co-ordinator of Research in Fictitious Numbers
(1981-1983)

Publications: Computers that Don't Count, *Journal of
Numbers, Science and Complicated Theories*, April 1979
Numbers and Machines, 1979
Integers: Real and Imaginary, 1981
The Science of Science, 1982.

INFORMATION SHEET

You are a member of the appointments committee for the
Department of Mathematics and Computing at Hardhit Polytechnic. The committee has to appoint a new lecturer. The
candidate must have three science A levels and a science degree
and must have good teaching experience, research experience
and administrative experience. Candidates should be young.

You have interviewed several candidates and have selected
the candidate below as the best of your interviewees. The
committee now has to choose which of the five different
candidates is the most suitable for the job.

[*Note:* To be a member of the Society of Countable Sciences
you must have two science A levels and a degree.]

Applicant: Mr Poirot
Age: 42
Nationality: Belgian
A levels: Mathematics, Physics, Biology, History
Qualifications: BSc in Mathematical Processing
Member of the Institute of Applied Numbers
Member of the Committee for Arbitrary Decisions
Certificate of Integerology (1980)
Member of the Society of Countable Sciences
MSc in Computing Studies

Experience: 5 years' teaching at Southurban University
2 years as an organizer of Southurban University
Maths Society
6 years as departmental adminsitrator

Publications: Random Thoughts on Random Numbers,
Journal of Numbers, Science and Complicated Theories,
Oct 1981

More Random Numbers, *Journal of Numbers, Science and Complicated Theories*, Nov 1982
Thinking about Mathematical Thinking, 1982.

INFORMATION SHEET

You are a member of the appointments committee for the Department of Mathematics and Computing at Hardhit Polytechnic. The committee has to appoint a new lecturer. The candidate must have three science A levels and a science degree and must have good teaching experience, research experience and administrative experience. Candidates should be young and a full member of the Institute of Applied Numbers.

You have interviewed several candidates and have selected the candidate below as the best of your interviewees. The committee now has to choose which of the five different candidates is the most suitable for the job.

[*Note:* To be a full member of the Institute of Applied Numbers you must have a Mathematics A level.]

> *Applicant:* Mr Edwards
> *Age:* 36
> *Nationality:* Nigerian
> *A levels:* Mathematics, Nuclear Physics, Greek, Computing
> *Qualifications:* BSc in Computer Engineering
>   Member of the Institute of Applied Numbers
>   Member of the Society of Countable Sciences
> *Experience:* 5 years' teaching at Idling University
>   14 years' administrative experience in various posts
>   ranging from treasurer of the National Numbers Group,
>   through Co-ordinator of the Work with Wobbly Integers
>   Project, to Head of Department, Faculty Chairman and
>   Assistant Vice Chancellor.

Supporting information for the tutor:
The exercise simulates the differential information available to any group discussion. It is important that the groups have five members and each member has a different application form and information sheet.

The problem can only be solved when the group realizes that the information they have is different for each group member and that all five members are needed to solve the problem.

Only two candidates are fully qualified for the post. Mr Abercrombie does not have the Certificate of Integerology,

Miss Bastaple is not a full member of the Institute of Applied Numbers because she lacks Mathematics A level (though she must have a science degree despite what her application form says) and Mr Poirot is too old. Of the two fully qualified candidates only Mrs Claus has a reasonable amount of teaching, research and administrative experience. Mr Edwards only has administrative experience. Students must combine resources to solve the problem and all group members must be involved. It is possible for the correct answer to be achieved in error so students should be asked to justify their decisions.

Discussion notes on groups:

The exercise can be used as a starting point for discussing group problem solving, stereotyping (as students' decisions may be prejudiced by the nationality or gender of applicants) or job applications. Discussion of group work should include:

1. Differential information — it is highly unlikely that members of a group will have the same information, attitudes and beliefs. The value of group discussion lies partly in bringing a number of different perspectives to bear. Efforts should always be made to bring all members of a group into the discussion and to discover the differences of opinion and background that may exist.
2. Problem solving is not merely a question of intuitive judgement or of logical movement from premise A to conclusion Z. It involves a degree of logic and a degree of evaluation and also the ability to step outside a closed problem and consider different aspects of it. This kind of problem cannot be solved by giving each member an individual task and breaking the overall decision down into individual tasks.
3. Any hostility or non-cooperation in a group will not only reduce the value of the experience for the hostile member(s) but also prevent the entire group from functioning effectively. Therefore, it is in the group's interest to involve all members. This is true of most group tasks.
4. A group may discover that a relatively easy way to attack the problem is to give all the sheets to one individual and let him/her tease out the logic. This can be used to illustrate the inappropriateness of the group to certain kinds of problem solving, such as purely logical tasks.

Supporting bibliography and references:

Argyle, M (1967) *The Psychology of Interpersonal Behaviour.* Penguin.
Bergin, F J (1976) *Practical Communication.* Pitman.
Dineen, J (1977) *Talking Your Way to Success.* Thorsons.
Goodworth, C T (1980) *Effective Speaking and Presentation for the Company Executive.* Hutchinson.

Variations:

The exercise can be incorporated into a longer project on interviewing and job applications by using five stooges to give the necessary information in interview. In this case the full exercise is best carried out in a half-day or full-day session in which the appointments committee must first decide on an interviewing strategy and hold the necessary interviews.

Topic 7: Theory of communication

Exercise 7.1

Information processing

Aims:

1. To give students practice in constructing algorithms;
2. To familiarize students with basic concepts in the communication process.

Equipment and materials required:
One copy of the 'A Model of Communication' paragraph for each student.

Time required:
The exercise requires five minutes' briefing, 30 minutes for creating the algorithms and 30 minutes of a subsequent session for discussion and lecture on information processing.

Procedure:
Brief the class and issue the paragraphs. When all students have constructed their algorithms collect them for evaluation and use them in a subsequent session as the basis for a lecture on information processing. Create a master algorithm using the best features of the students' work and then ask them to add items which are missing from the model or the original paragraph.

125

Discuss the application of the model to communicative processes other than conversation, such as a committee, letter writing, newspapers, television advertising, human-computer interaction and teaching.

Information for the students:
Briefing:

> Below is a paragraph describing the fundamental features of communication as found in a normal two-person communication. Draw an algorithm or flow chart which contains all the elements of the communication process as described here. Make sure that all stages are contained and the order in which they occur is indicated.

'A MODEL OF COMMUNICATION – CONVERSATION'

To work properly any conversation must have at least two participants, one speaker who is sending a message and one listener who is receiving it. The conversation will be about some topic, expressing a thought or emotion of the speaker/sender and the symbols which are used to encode that thought or feeling. Those symbols may also refer to something other than the thought or feeling intended by the speaker. The speaker must use various vocal organs to express his meaning and thus transmit the message in some form. This may be further transmitted by telephone, radio, record, tape, microphone and so on. Similarly, the listener may use devices to receive the message but ultimately it reaches his/her ears and is decoded by the brain and stored in memory.

Supporting information for the tutor:
If the students have no experience of flow charts or algorithms a lecture should be given acquainting them with the principles. The exercise can be used as their first practice of those principles.

An algorithm is essentially a structured, sequenced, logical model of a process. Algorithms can be written in English as a series of statements describing processes and conditional tests, such as:

1. The speaker selects a message by selecting a thought and/or emotion.
2. If there are different symbols available for encoding the chosen message then the speaker selects appropriate symbols.
3. The speaker encodes the message in symbols.
4. The speaker activates vocal organs.
5. If there are different possible media for transmission then the speaker chooses a suitable medium.

6. The speaker transmits signals through the chosen medium.

Some computing languages enable algorithms to be described in this fashion. If students have computing experience they might be asked to translate an English-like algorithm into a computing language of their choice.

A flow chart represents information in a similar form but employs visual structuring as well as verbal counters. The simplest flow charts consist of rectangular boxes for processes and diamond-shaped boxes for decisions. A process box must only have one exit point. A decision box must have two. Complex decisions and complex processes must be broken down into their discrete components in order to fit the representation and thus to reveal their logical structure. More complex flow charts identify boxes of different kinds, for example a box for input of new information into the system and a box for the printing of output information. An example is shown in Figure 4.

The resulting algorithms or flow charts should not only follow the rules of a well constructed analysis, containing logical chunks in logical sequence, but it should also contain all the following elements:

1. Sender
2. Receiver
3. Message to be transmitted
4. Encoding
5. Means of transmission (several choices of physical medium)
6. Symbols transmitted
7. Reference of symbols
8. Symbols received
9. Means of decoding
10. Message received
11. Message store.

Elements which should emerge from discussion to be added to the model but which are not mentioned in the paragraph are:

1. Initial message store from which the speaker extracts the message.
2. *Noise.* Interference in the system which corrupts the symbols. This may enter the process at several points, notably psychological and physiological processes of sending (such as stammering), interference in transmission (such as electrical interference on a telephone line or talking in a lecture) and psychological and physiological processes of reception (such as deafness or perceptual distortion).

127

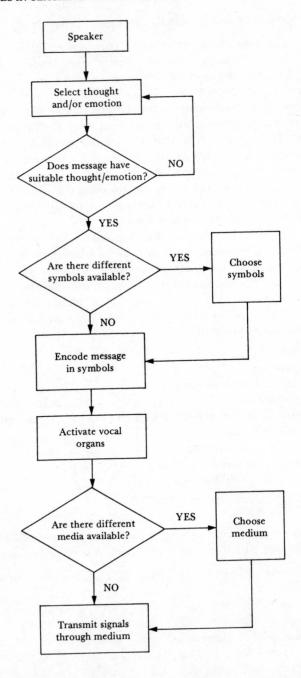

Figure 4. *Example flow chart*

3. *Redundancy.* Where there is noise in a communications system there will be redundancy in the signals intended to combat that noise. Signals may be repeated or employ more complex forms of redundancy. (To explore this, exercise 7.3 can be run immediately after this exercise.)
4. *Feedback.* There is communication between both participants in a conversation, even if one person does not speak. NVC signals interest, attention, assent and so on, giving the speaker feedback on the level of understanding of the listener. The process described in the paragraph is two-way in most conversations.

Supporting bibliography and references:
Bergin, F J (1976) *Practical Communication.* Pitman
Cherry, C (1957) *On Human Communication.* MIT Press.

Variations:

1. If no lecture is to be given the exercise can usefully be extended by pairing students off and asking them to combine the best features of both algorithms in each pair. Then pairs can be formed into groups of four to consider what may be missing from the descriptions prior to class discussion.
2. Ask students to think of another typical communicative situation, such as a radio news broadcast, and to create a similar flow chart. Then the flow charts for both processes can be compared and evaluated.

Exercise 7.2

Language, grammar and algorithms

Aims:

1. To give students practice in analysing language structures;
2. To give students practice in algorithm design;
3. To illustrate the relationships between language and algorithms.

Equipment and materials required:
One copy of the 'Sample Sentences' sheet for each student.

Time required:
The exercise requires ten minutes' briefing, and between one

and three hours to carry out, depending on the linguistic experience of the groups. Up to 30 minutes can be reserved for discussion of the resulting models.

Procedure:
Brief the class and divide them into groups of between four and six members. Issue the 'Sample Sentences' sheets to all students. Each group then must create a model of the language used in the sentences. When all groups are satisfied that they have an accurate model the algorithms should be exchanged between groups. Then each group generates sentences using the model it has been given, in order to test its accuracy. Where odd sentences are produced the rules which led to the oddity should be identified. In the final discussion the reasons for these problems can be examined.

Information to the students:
Briefing:

> You have been given a set of sentences of English. Your task is to produce a model, grammar or algorithm (or all three) which will generate those sentences and other similar sentences of English. The model must contain the vocabulary and the grammatical rules which are needed to produce these sentences.

SAMPLE SENTENCES

1. The man was in London.
2. A child read the red book.
3. The woman liked an old artist.
4. Our cat saw the big dog and the dog came after Mr Smith.
5. Napoleon was from Corsica.
6. I ran by the river.
7. The old dog never ran after the cat.
8. They saw an old man and he always walked to London.
9. She ran sometimes.
10. My cat never liked Napoleon but he liked Corsica always.

Categories of words you might try to identify include nouns, proper nouns, verbs, adverbs, adjectives, conjunctions, pronouns, prepositions and determiners.

Supporting information for the tutor:
Students require some knowledge of syntax, rewrite rules or algorithms to tackle this task adequately. The sentences contain the following vocabulary:

1. Determiners — a, an, the

2. Prepositions — in, from, after, to, by
3. Conjunctions — and, but
4. Adverbs — never, always, sometimes
5. Pronouns — I, she, they
6. Adjectives — my, your, his, our, red, old, big
7. Nouns — man, book, woman, cat, dog, river, child, artist
8. Proper nouns — London, Mr Smith, Napoleon, Corsica
9. Verbs — was, ran, liked, saw, read, came, walked.

The grammatical rules used are:

Rule 1: Sentence — NP + VP + (conjunction + S)
Rule 2: NP — [proper noun
             — pronoun
             — (determiner) + (adjective) + noun]
Rule 3: VP — [(adverb) + verb (+ NP)
             — verb + (adverb) (+ NP) (+ preposition + NP)]

( ) signifies optional items
[ ] signifies a list of possible choices, one of which must
    be made.

You should ensure that all these rules and the whole vocabulary is included in the resultant models. Discuss with students the difficulties of analysing the sentences and drawing up such models. Get students to explore the difference between a syntactically correct sentence and a semantically correct sentence by generating different sentences from the models. Ask for suggestions for improvement of the models. If time permits discuss ways that the main difficulties (which will be semantic) can be overcome.

Supporting bibliography and references:
Crystal, D (1976) *Linguistics.* Penguin.

Variations:

1. For students who are being taught programming this exercise can be extended. Once students have created their grammar or algorithm they can be asked to turn it into a program which generates sentences. This has proved a useful exercise for computing students as it demonstrates some of the similarities and differences between natural and formal languages.

2. *School variation*
   Algorithms and formal grammar may be of little value to

pupils at an introductory level. However, an awareness of the fact that language has an inherent structure and is a set of rules can be useful knowledge when considering, for example, the nature of written style or ambiguity.

The set of sentences given can still be used in an attempt to find 'words of the same type' and 'words of different types'. For example, ask pupils to substitute words from one sentence in other sentences and then decide:

(a) Does the new sentence make sense? If not, what has changed to make it nonsense?
(b) Could you imagine a situation in which the new sentence made sense?
(c) Even if it does not make sense, do you think it is grammatical?

It is easy to move from questions such as these to the differences between meaning (or 'content') and form; to talk about full or content words which have meaning independent of any sentence they are used in and words which only have syntactic function (the so called 'function' words); and to consider the differences between acceptable and unacceptable, grammatical and ungrammatical and formal and informal sentences. Pupils may even derive syntactic categories such as noun, verb and preposition by the kinds of substitution they find which make 'some kind of sense'.

■ Exercise 7.3

Redundancy

Aims:

1. To give students practice in analysing text;
2. To introduce students to the concept of redundancy in communication;
3. To encourage students to recognize the need for non-factual information in normal communication.

Equipment and materials required:
One copy of the 'Redundancy' sheet for each student.

Time required:
Approximately five minutes will be required for the briefing.

Allow about 20 minutes for conducting the exercise and 15 minutes for plenary commentary.

Procedure:

Issue a copy of the 'Redundancy' sheet to each student and describe the task. Point out that the missing items are not just words but parts of words and groups of words.

Information for the students:

The following text has been written in normal English but several items have been omitted. Fill in the blanks by guessing the missing items and then answer these questions:

1. How did you know the item or type of item that was missing? What information or evidence are you paying attention to?
2. Are there different categories of item in your list? For example, are all the missing items words? Is evidence of the same kind being used to guess all of these types?
3. If you are able to guess all the missing items with virtual certainty why do you think those items would normally be used? What is the point of such superfluous information?
4 Are there alternatives for any of the slots?

REDUNDANCY: TEXT

The - ueen of Sheba was sitting on the - - - - - -. On her head she wore - c - - - -. She hummed - - - - -. 'Hickory Dickory Dock,
- - -   - - - - -   - - -   - - - - -   - - - - -'. There was - knock on the
- - - -. 'Come - -', she sa - d. - peasant came - - and made a - - -.
'- - - - - - - - - want?' - - - q - - - - - - - -. 'Your - - - - - - -', - - - -
- - - peasant 'The peasant -   - - - revolt - - -'. 'Never - - - -', - - - -
- - - queen 'The q - - - - - - S - - - - rules, - -'.

Supporting information for the tutor:

NOTES ON REDUNDANCY

Redundancy occurs in almost all forms of communication to combat the noise which can enter a communication system. The greater the likelihood of noise, the greater the need for redundancy. In language it occurs at all levels. The text includes lexical, phrasal, semantic and graphological (or phonological) redundancy.

Methods of creating redundancy:

1. Repeat the same message using the same symbols and the same channel of communication (eg 'Come in number four your time is up. Come in number four').
2. Repeat the same message using different symbols but the

133

same channel (eg 'It's time for me to go. I'll just put my coat on and then I'll be off. My wife will be wondering where I am and it's getting late').

3. Repeat the same message using different symbols and different channels (eg saying 'No' while shaking your head).

The amount of redundancy in a system or signal is related to the amount of information conveyed. The more redundancy there is the less information there will be. Information is thus a probabilistic notion. The more uncertain the next symbol or message (ie the more choices there are available in the system) the more information is conveyed by the actual choice that is made. If a symbol or message is totally predictable (such as the 'u' following a 'q') no additional information is conveyed.

Supporting bibliography and references:
Cherry, C (1957) *On Human Communication.* MIT Press.

Variations:

1. A short lecture may be needed before or after the exercise to familiarize students with the related concepts of noise and redundancy. This can be further reinforced by using exercise 7.1 shortly after this exercise.

2. Use the exercise as an introduction to work on the structure of language. Spotting the redundancy in the sample text involves recognizing linguistic features at various levels of analysis.

3. Follow the exercise up by asking students to list different forms of communication and attempt to rank them in order of the amount of redundancy in the system. Possible inclusions could be — semaphore, morse code, telephone conversations, a Barbara Cartland romance, a James Joyce novel, a physics textbook, the label on a bottle, a political speech, a newspaper advertisement, a lecture.

■ Exercise 7.4

The functions of language

Aims:

1. To encourage students to consider the range of uses to which language can be put;

2. To show that conveying information is not the most important of language functions;
3. To introduce students to the idea that 'meanings' can exist at levels other than the purely factual, such as social and cultural meaning;
4. To persuade students that verbal communication is not simply a matter of stating facts.

Equipment and materials required:
Chalkboard, students' collections of sample texts.

Time required:
Approximately five minutes will be required for the briefing. Allow at least ten minutes for each of the following stages plus a further 20 minutes for plenary discussion of the results.

Procedure:

1. Each student must bring a written text to the session. This may be any form of written text including transcripts of spoken text, advertisements, poetry, news reports, lecture notes.
2. Each student passes the given text to his/her neighbour.
3. The student must then take the given text and:
   (a) Strike out all phrases which are definitely and only statements of fact and serve no other purpose in the text. Record the number of deletions.
   (b) Write out the remaining text one element at a time in a column on the left of a page.
   (c) Against each element of the text on the right-hand side briefly state why that element is in the text — its function or purpose or the intention of the author.
   Students are then arranged into small groups and must attempt to arrange the notes they have made into a list of 'functions of language'. In doing so they should also note any marked differences between the function lists for different types of text.
      The tutor should then draw a collective list of lists by extracting comments from all groups.

Information for the students:
Briefing:

On the text in front of you delete any phrases which you think are purely factual and serve no purpose in the text other than to convey facts. When you have deleted all such phrases count up the number of deletions and write a list of the remaining phrases on the left-hand

135

side of a clean sheet of paper. Against this column of phrases write on the right-hand side a brief explanation of why that phrase is in the text, what it is doing or what its function is.

When you have done this you will join a small group to pool your results. Try to produce a complete list of all the functions language can have, based on the texts you have just analysed. Try also to establish what differences of function exist in the different texts your group has examined.

Supporting information for the tutor:

NOTES ON FUNCTIONS OF LANGUAGE

It is unlikely that all the major functions of language will emerge from the basic exercise, though they may be drawn out in the plenary session. The main functions that should emerge, as listed by Robinson, are:

1. Avoidance of other problems (using language to hide embarrassment, confusion or ignorance).
2. Conformity to norms (using particular forms of language because they are generally used by others in similar situations or because such use is expected of someone in the given situation).
3. Aesthetics (literary use of language, but also humour, crosswords and all other forms of word play for its own sake).
4. Encounter regulation (greetings, leave-takings and other devices for controlling social encounters).
5. Performatives (language used to perform an action which cannot be performed without that particular use of language, such as betrothal, vowing, promising, swearing).
6. Regulation of self (talking to oneself, as a means of rehearsal or self-control).
7. Regulation of others (attempting to control the behaviour of others through direct commands or more complex social control).
8. Expression of affect (conveying an attitude).
9. Marking of emitter
   (a) emotional state (unconsciously betraying the current emotional state of a speaker)
   (b) personality (language as containing social information, regional information and personal idiolect).
10. Role relationship marking (establishing and maintaining power relationships, treating other participants in an exchange as stereotypes).

11. Reference (talking about things, ostension).
12. Instruction (giving new information, using languages as part of a physical demonstration).
13. Inquiry (requesting information).
14. Metalanguage (using language to talk about language).

Supporting bibliography and references:
Robinson, W P (1972) *Language and Social Behaviour.* Penguin.

Variations:

1. As the exercise depends on a variety of texts, an alternative to asking students to bring their own texts is to choose a preselected set of examples.

2. To include spoken texts in the discussion build the exercise around clips from films, TV advertisements, radio broadcasts, political speeches and scripts. Students can be sent to a cloakroom, restaurant, street or other public place immediately before the session to record actual conversations.

Using Exercises in Teaching Communication

Introduction

There is no set way in which the exercises in this book should be included in a course. In order to decide how and when to use the exercises, it is necessary for the tutor to analyse the particular situation or context in which the course occurs. Important among the factors to be considered are:

— the communication aims of the course;
— tutor expertise (in communication and other subjects);
— student details (eg number, level, age, experience);
— academic context (eg other subjects studied);
— length of course (eg number and length of sessions);
— assessment required.

The courses and 'modules' (parts of courses) outlined in this section demonstrate how the exercises can be used successfully in a variety of settings.

School modules

A module on written communication for school

Pupils may finish their schooling with a relatively narrow experience of written communication and understanding of language. If they are arts or humanities students they may have extensive essay writing skills but little in the way of report writing or other formal written communication. If they are science or technical students they are likely to have an even narrower experience of writing. There are many ways that exercises within this book can be combined to increase the written skills of such students. The following module is one possibility.

Communication aims:

1. To familiarize students with a variety of forms of

written presentation;

2. To sensitize students to some of the main factors to consider when writing;
3. To encourage students to apply principles and system to their formal writing;
4. To give students practice in written communication skills.

Suitable for: pupils with little training in report writing or written English
Number of sessions: eight
Session time: one hour
Number of students: up to 30
Tutor's expertise: Knowledge of rules of basic English required
Assessment: Written report

Outline of the sessions:

1. Exercise 2.8 'Some common problems in written communication'. Mini-lecture and discussion on ambiguity and rules in written English.

2. Exercise 7.2 'Language, grammar and algorithms'. Use variant 2 to develop notions of the rules of language.

3. Exercise 2.6 'Styles of language'. This exercise can be used to illustrate the relationship between the rules of language established in the previous exercise and different ways of writing.

4. Exercise 2.7 'Readability and style'. Pupils now begin to consider the practicalities of writing well by exploring the idea of readability and how it may be achieved.

5. Exercise 2.1 'Effective presentation'. Use this exercise to place the ideas students have developed about language in the context of formal structured writing.

6. Exercise 3.7 'Developing a point'. This exercise could optionally be introduced here to encourage pupils to attempt specific techniques for presenting information (primarily using language). Make the point that many of the principles of written and oral presentation are the same.

7. Exercise 2.2 'An investigation report'. Finally, students are asked to prepare a report for assessment using this exercise. Use one of the topics suggested in variant 3.
   — Problem definition and preparation.

139

8. Exercise 2.2 (continued). Give a second section over to the task of writing the report so that groups can assign roles.
   — Writing the report (to be completed as homework).

A research project in communication skills — improving the image of the school

Where motivation is a problem or the pupils represent a wide range of backgrounds and interests, it is often best to build a course around the characteristics a tutor is certain they all possess. A sensible topic area is therefore the school itself and, as most pupils are very media conscious, the notion of publicizing the school can be highly motivating.

Ideally a course such as that outlined here would be supported by actual input from the local media, perhaps by visits to a local radio station or a talk given by a local journalist. However, as a 'simulation' of investigative research such glamour is unnecessary.

Scenario: Pupils are to form groups and decide on ways that they can improve the public image of their school. This involves searching the library for information, gathering information and opinions from other pupils and staff, being interviewed by the 'media' about their school and finally giving a 'public' talk about the school which is intended to attract more pupils and support.

Communication aims:

1. To encourage students to pursue a sustained and varied research project in communication;
2. To enable students to practise a range of interpersonal and communicative skills;
3. To encourage students to apply principles of communication to their normal communicative behaviour;
4. To sensitize students to different forms of communication and the variations in presentation skills required;
5. To give students some confidence in their own communicative abilities;
6. To introduce students to group work.

Suitable for: any pupils over the age of 11 years
Number of sessions: 11
Session time: one hour
Number of students: 15 to 30

Tutor's expertise: Knowledge of basic communication is
   required and some interest in media, especially community
   media, is desirable.
Assessment: Oral presentation.

Outline of the sessions:

1. Exercise 6.1 'Introduction to group work'.
   Topic — Improving the image of the school. Pupils should
   be asked to produce lists of ways the school's image could
   be improved, perhaps through presenting the school better
   or by actually changing some aspects of it.

2. Exercise 1.1 'Library search: annotating a reading list'.
   Replace the Elaskay topic with 'The media and education'.
   Pupils must identify material which can help to change the
   school's image. Such material will be either about education
   and public attitudes or about the nature of information, the
   media and presentation. Ensure that newspapers and
   magazines are searched as these may be major sources of
   relevant ideas.

3. Exercise 6.3 'Decision making'. After running the exercise
   ask each group to evaluate and rank its lists of information
   and ideas on image presenting.

4. Exercise 4.1 'Introduction to interpersonal communication'.
   Present the media interview within the following scenario:
   The media have discovered that the pupils of the school are
   worried about its image and so want to find out from one
   of those pupils exactly what is wrong with the school.
   The pupil being interviewed wants to ensure, on the other
   hand, that he or she conveys as good an image of the
   school as possible.

5. Exercise 4.2 'Questioning skills'. Attention now turns to
   discovering what pupils and staff in general think about the
   school and its image. Use this exercise to enable pupils to
   develop questioning technique and confidence.

6. Exercise 5.1 'Information-gathering interviews'. Instead of
   constructing this exercise around the idea of a computing
   consultancy team, ask the pupils to construct an interview
   for a member of staff (or pupil if no staff member is
   available) to find out more about the school and others'
   opinions of it. Ideally the interview(s) will be carried out
   on staff and students not involved in the project. If this is

141

not possible then the tutor should be interviewed by each group and each group should be allowed to conduct the same interview on one or two other pupils in the class.

7. Exercise 5.1 (continued). Carrying out the interviews.

8. Exercise 3.2 'Preparing for an oral presentation'. Groups are now told they are to present a talk using the information they have discovered. The talk is for parents whose children will soon be old enough to enter the school. Journalists have also been invited to the talk. Use this exercise to structure their information for such a talk.

9. Exercise 3.4 'The systematic approach to oral presentation'. Each group must give a talk which aims to improve the school's image, based on the information it has obtained. This is the scenario for the exercise.
   — Preparing the talk.

10. Exercise 3.4 (continued). Giving the talk. Each group presents its talk to the other groups who act as the audience. The audience are allowed to question the presenters. If video-recording facilities are not available to facilitate stage 2 then all members of the audience should be asked to evaluate each presentation using the criteria given in the exercise.

11. Exercise 3.4 (continued). Evaluating the presentation. Each group's presentation is evaluated using the judgements made by the audience. Ideally this session should immediately follow the previous one so that impressions are not lost. This is especially the case if the talks have not been recorded on video.

An introductory module on written and oral presentation

This module is designed to be used at the very beginning of the students' higher education. As well as introducing the students to essential written and oral skills, it also helps them to form social and working groups.

Communication aims:

1. To help students to mix, form groups and gain confidence early in their course;
2. To introduce them to some of the difficulties faced by groups in solving problems;

3. To guide them through a systematic approach to problem solving;
4. To encourage them to apply this approach to the problems of writing reports and preparing talks.

Suitable for: first year degree and diploma students on any course
Number of sessions: eight
Session time: one hour
Number of students: 20 to 30
Tutor's expertise: Basic knowledge of communication required
Assessment: 1. Written report
　　　　　　　　2. Oral presentation.

Outline of the sessions:

1. Exercise 2.1 'Effective presentation' (35 minutes). Lecture on 'The Systematic Approach to Report Writing'.

2. Exercise 2.2 'An investigation report'.
   — Topic — effectiveness of Freshers' Week
   — Define the problem (15 minutes)
   — Consider the content of the report (15 minutes)
   — Prepare a short questionnaire (30 minutes)
   Homework — collect information.

3. Exercise 2.2 (continued).
   — Interpreting information
   — Assigning writing tasks
   — Writing the parts of the report.

4. Exercise 2.2 (continued).
   — Completing the report.

5. Exercise 3.1 'Giving instructions' (15 minutes).
   Exercise 3.2 'Preparing for an oral presentation'.
   — Lecture on 'brain patterns' (10 minutes)
   — Production of a 'brain pattern' (20 minutes)
   — Discussion of 'patterns' by all the class (10 minutes)
   Homework — preparation for next week's short talks.

6. Exercise 3.4 'The systematic approach to oral presentation'.
   — Topic — effectiveness of Freshers' Week
   — Briefing and preliminaries (15 minutes)
   — Deciding the content (15 minutes)
   — Preparing the content (30 minutes).

7. Exercise 3.4 (continued).
   — Preparing the introduction (10 minutes)
   — Preparing the conclusion (10 minutes)
   — Presentations and evaluations (40 minutes).

8. Exercise 3.4 (continued).
   — Presentations and evaluations (50 minutes)
   — Discussion (10 minutes).

Selection interviews

It is advantageous to deal with the skills of interviewing and being interviewed in the same series of exercises. When students play the roles of interviewers and interviewees, the learning experiences of one aspect can often be utilized in the other. Also, by using an appropriate series, savings can be made in student and staff time.

A module on selection interviews

This module is designed for those communication courses which are restricted to one hour per week. It is more effective if used fairly late in the students' higher education.

Communication aims:

1. To give the students advice and practice in applying for jobs;
2. To provide a framework in which students can tackle the problems of interviewing and being interviewed;
3. To give students advice and practice in structuring selection interviews;
4. To give students practice in the skills required by interviewers;
5. To give students advice and practice in being interviewed.

Suitable for: first year degree and diploma students on any course
Number of sessions: ten
Session time: one hour
Number of students: 20 to 30
Tutor's expertise: basic knowledge of communication required

Outline of the sessions:

1. Exercise 1.2 'Library search: abstracts and summaries'.

— Briefing
— Completion of exercise in the library.

2. Exercise 2.4 'Applying for a job: preparation' (35 minutes)
   Lecture on 'Writing a CV' (15 minutes)
   Homework — writing a curriculum vitae.

3. Exercise 2.5 'Writing a curriculum vitae and a covering letter'.

4. Exercise 4.1 'Introduction to interpersonal communication'.
   — Recording of interviews (20 minutes)
   — Replay and discussion (40 minutes).

5. Lecture on 'The objectives, structure and process of selection interviewing'.
   Exercise 5.3 'The structure of selection interviews'.
   — Preparation by interviewing teams.

6. Exercise 5.3 (continued).
   — Recording of two interviews concentrating on structure
   — Replay and discussion of key parts.

7. Exercise 5.4 'Interviewer skills in selection interviews'.
   — Recording of two interviews concentrating on skills
   — Replay and discussion of key parts.

8. Exercise 5.5 'Thinking about being interviewed'.

9. Exercise 5.6 'Interviewee skills in selection interviews'.
   — Recording of two interviews
   — Replay and discussion of key parts.

10. Exercise 5.6 (continued).
    — Recording of two interviews
    — Replay and discussion of key parts.

A two-day course on selection interviews

Although it is possible to deal with selection interviewing on a one- or two-hour per week basis over several weeks, considerable gains can be made if the training is carried out for full days. The short course outlined below has been used successfully for several years.

Communication aims:

1. To provide a framework in which students can tackle the problems of interviewing and being interviewed.

145

2. To give students advice and practice in structuring selection interviews;
3. To give students practice in the skills required by interviewers;
4. To give students advice and practice in being interviewed.

Suitable for: any students over 16 years; particularly useful for mature groups
Number of sessions: two sessions + two days
Number of students: 10 to 15
Tutor's expertise: Knowledge and experience of interviewing required
Before the course: Students complete exercises 2.5 and 2.6

Timetable for day 1: 'Interviewing'

9.30 Introduction to the course

9.35 Exercise 4.1 'Introduction to interpersonal communication'.
   — Briefing and preparation (10 minutes);
   — Recording of 'television interviews' (15 minutes);
   — Playback and discussion (15 minutes).

10.15 Coffee

10.30 Exercise 5.3 'The structure of selection interviews'.
   — Lecture on the structure of selection interviews;
   — Preparation by interview teams (20 minutes);
   — Recording of two interviews (40 minutes);
   — Playback and discussion (60 minutes).

12.30 Lunch

1.30 Lecture 'Interviewer skills'

1.50 Exercise 4.2 'Questioning skills'.

2.30 Exercise 5.4 'Interviewer skills in selection interviews'.
   — Preparation by interview teams + tea (20 minutes);
   — Recording of two interviews (40 minutes);
   — Playback and discussion (60 minutes).

4.30 End of day 1.

Timetable for day 2: 'Being interviewed'

9.30 Exercise 5.5 'Thinking about being interviewed'.
   — Create guidelines for being interviewed;
   — Present guidelines for discussion.

10.15 Coffee

10.30 Exercise 5.6 'Interviewee skills in selection interviews'.
— Preparation by interview teams (15 minutes);
— Recording of three interviews (45 minutes);
— Playback and discussion (60 minutes).

12.30 Lunch

1.30 Exercise 5.6 'Interviewee skills in selection interviews'.
— Preparation by interview teams (15 minutes);
— Recording of three interviews (45 minutes);
— Playback and discussion (60 minutes).

3.30 Tea

3.45 Discussion — how to enhance one's chances for the job?

4.30 End of course.

Using a science-based exercise

By using science-based exercises to provide the content of a communication studies course, it is possible to overcome the problems of relevance and motivation noted in Section A. Many of the exercises (case studies, games, simulations) given in Ellington *et al.* (1981) are suitable for adaptation and use in this way. The rationale is illustrated by Marshall *et al.* (1982) in two examples. In one, 'Proteins as human food' (Percival, 1977), the case study provides the basis for an exercise on communication and decision making in groups. In the other, a case study about alternative energy is used as the focal point of a whole communication studies course. The latter, which is outlined below, has been used successfully at Sheffield City Polytechnic since 1979 with, on average, 200 engineering and science students per year.

The alternative energy programme

Communication aims:

1. To encourage organized literature searching;
2. To introduce students to some of the difficulties faced by groups in solving problems and making decisions;
3. To guide students through a systematic approach to problem solving;

147

4. To encourage students to apply this approach to the
   problems of writing reports and preparing talks.

Suitable for: A level, first year degree and diploma students
   taking engineering or science
Number of sessions: ten
Session time: two hours
Number of students: 20 to 30
Tutor's expertise: basic knowledge of science and
   communication required
Assessment: 1. Library exercise
                2. Written report
                3. Oral presentation.

Outline of the sessions:

1. *Introduction to the communication studies course:*
   In this first session, the lecturer explains the communication
   studies course to the class. The students then work in pairs
   and in small groups to complete exercise 6.1 ('Introduction
   to group work'). In this exercise, the students in each group
   list and evaluate alternative sources of energy, and also
   reflect on their group's performance in tackling the task.
   The session ends with an outline of the rest of the
   programme.

2. *Introduction to the library:*
   The students are given the briefing sheet for exercise 1.1
   ('Library search: annotating a reading list'), asking them
   to produce an annotated list of materials on one source of
   alternative energy. They are then given an introductory
   tour of the library before completing the exercise.

3. *Preparation for the group talk:*
   After a brief lecture on using 'brain patterns' (Buzan,
   1982), the class is divided into groups and asked to
   complete exercise 3.2 ('Preparing for an oral presentation').
   In the second half of the session, the groups are told to
   prepare a ten-minute talk on alternative energy, as given in
   the brief for exercise 3.5 ('A group talk on alternative
   energy'). The students should be able to complete the bulk
   of stages 1 and 2 of this exercise before the end of the
   session.

4. *Giving the group talk:*
In this session, the groups complete stages 3 and 4 of exercise 3.5, viz. giving and evaluating their talks.

5. *Writing a report:*
The students are given a lecture on the systematic approach to problem solving with specific reference to report writing. The groups are then asked to write a report (using the same brief as for the group talk) following the guidelines set out in exercise 2.2 ('An investigation report').

6. *Decision making:*
After a brief lecture on the importance of creativity and effective utilization of resources in group work, the students are asked individually to complete the task specified in exercise 6.3 ('Decision making'). In the second part of the session, the published case study *Power for Elaskay* (Ellington and Addinall, 1978) is introduced, and time given for the students to read some of the preparatory material.

7. *Power for Elaskay:*
At this point in the course, the technical material from *Power for Elaskay* is used to provide information about using alternative energy on the Island of Elaskay. The class is divided into five groups, and each group is provided with data relating to one of the following sources of energy: solar, wind, tidal, hydroelectric, and peat. Using this data to complete the worksheets provided in the published package, each group is able to calculate the technical and economic feasibility of using their source. Each group is then asked to produce a list of about five advantages and disadvantages in using their source of energy.

8. *Devising the rolling programme:*
The class is divided into teams of 'consultants' such that each team contains at least one 'expert' on each of the five sources of energy. Each team is then asked to devise a rolling programme to meet the island's electricity requirements over the next 50 years. In designing this programme, the teams utilize the information gathered from the previous sessions and from the material contained in the published package.

9. *Preparation of the oral presentation:*
Each team prepares a short (ten-minute) presentation of

149

their rolling programme for the islanders of Elaskay. The lecturer guides the teams through the stages of preparation given in exercise 3.4 ('The systematic approach to oral presentation').

10. *Presentation and discussion of the rolling programme:* Each team presents and defends its rolling programme to the 'islanders' (the remaining students). After all the teams have presented their programmes, each one is evaluated on the basis of presentation (using the evaluation checklist given in exercise 3.4) and content.

Bibliography

Abt, C C (1968) Games for learning. In Boocock, S S and Schild, O E *Simulation Games in Learning*, pp.65-84. Sage Publications, Beverley Hills.

Albright, R J and Albright, L G (1981) Developing professional qualities in engineering students. *Engineering Education*, April.

Appell, A L (1984) *A Practical Approach to Human Behaviour in Business*. Charles E Merrill, Columbus, Ohio.

Argyle, M (1967) *The Psychology of Interpersonal Behaviour*. Penguin.

Bergin, F J (1976) *Practical Communication*. Pitman.

Blanchard, B and Marshall, S (1980) A case study in industrial and communication studies. *International Journal of Mechanical Engineering Education*, 8:3.

Bloomer, J (1973) What have simulation and gaming got to do with programmed learning and educational technology? *Programmed Learning & Educational Technology*, 10:4.

Boocock, S S and Schild, O E (1968) *Simulation Games in Learning*. Sage Publications, Beverley Hills.

Bufton, I, Aram, J and Roberts, L (1983) *Applications and Interviews*. AGCAS Careers Information Booklet. Central Services Unit for University and Polytechnic Careers and Appointment Services (CSU).

Buzan, T (1982) *Using Your Head*. BBC Publications.

CBI (1976) reported in 'Education and training', Third Report from the Select Committee on Science and Technology. HMSO.

Cherry, C (1957) *On Human Communication*. MIT Press.

Cooper, B (1964) *Writing Technical Reports*. Penguin.

Crystal, D (1976) *Linguistics.* Penguin.

Deverell, C S (1973) *Successful Communication.* G Bell & Sons.

Dineen, J (1977) *Talking Your Way to Success.* Thorsons.

Ellington, H I and Addinall, E (1978) *Power for Elaskay.* The Institution of Electrical Engineers, London.

Ellington, H I, Addinall, E and Percival, F (1981) *Games and Simulations in Science Education.* Kogan Page, London.

Finniston, M (1980) Engineering our future. Report of the Committee of Enquiry into the Engineering Profession. HMSO.

Fisher, Cassie W and Constantine, T (1977) *Student's Guide to Success.* Macmillan, London.

Garvey, D M (1971) Simulation: a catalogue of judgements, findings, and hunches. In Tansey, P J (ed) *Educational Aspects of Simulation*, 204-227. McGraw-Hill, London.

Gibbs, G I (ed) (1974) *Handbook of Games and Simulation Exercises.* E & F N Spon, London.

Goodworth, C T (1980) *Effective Speaking and Presentation for the Company Executive.* Hutchinson.

Gray, T G F (1979) Between-the-lines teaching of communication skills in an engineering course. Conference on Language and Communication Skills Instruction in Scientific and Engineering Education, Sheffield City Polytechnic.

Gray, T G F (1981) Communication skills in engineering. *Chartered Mechanical Engineer,* April.

Hall, J and Watson, W H (1970) The effects of normative intervention on group decision-making performance. *Human Relations,* 23:4.

Hargie, O, Saunders, C and Dickson, D (1981) *Social Skills in Interpersonal Communication.* Croom Helm, London.

Hills, P J, Gardiner, P F and McVey, P J (1979) Communication skills (results of a survey of books, materials and courses in universities, polytechnics and Institutes of Higher Education in the United Kingdom). University of Surrey, Guildford.

Hills, P and Gilbert, J (eds) (1977) *Aspects of Educational Technology XI.* Kogan Page, London.

Kincaid, J P and Delionbach, L J (1973) Validation of the automated readability index: a follow-up. *Human Factors*, 15:1.

Kirkman, J (1980) *Good Style for Scientific and Engineering Writing*. Pitman.

Marshall, S (1981) Communication studies: an alternative programme. *International Journal of Electrical Engineering Education*, 18:4.

Marshall, S (1982) Relevance and motivation in communication studies courses for engineering students. *European Journal of Engineering Education*, 7.

Marshall, S, Ellington, H I, Addinall, E and Percival, F (1982) Developing communication skills using simulation/gaming techniques. *Simulation/Games for Learning*, 12:2.

Maude, B (1974) *Practical Communication for Managers*. Longman.

Palmer, R and Pope, C (1984) *Brain Train: Studying for Success*. E & F N Spon, London.

Percival, F (1977) The development and evaluation of a structured scientific communication exercise. In Hills, P and Gilbert, J (eds) *Aspects of Educational Technology XI*. Kogan Page, London.

Percival, F and Ellington, H I (1980) The place of case studies in the simulation/gaming field. In Race, P and Brook, D (eds) *Perspectives on Academic Gaming and Simulation 5*, 21-30. Kogan Page, London.

Race, P and Brook, D (eds) (1980) *Perspectives on Academic Gaming and Simulation 5*. Kogan Page, London.

Railton, D (1984) *Approaches Towards Technical Communication Skills Training in British Higher Education*. Language Studies Unit Research Report, The University of Aston in Birmingham.

Robinson, W P (1972) *Language and Social Behaviour*. Penguin.

Smithson, S (1984) *Business Communication Today*. ICSA Publishing, Cambridge.

Stanton, N (1982) *The Business of Communicating*. Pan, London.

Stanton, N (1982) *What Do You Mean 'Communication'?* Pan, London.

Tansey, P J (ed) (1971) *Educational Aspects of Simulation.* McGraw-Hill, London.

Van den Berghe, W (1983) *General Education in University-Level Professional Studies.* Interim Report on part of the Industry-University Action-Research and Evaluation Program. Industry-University Foundation, Brussels, Belgium.

Vardaman, G T (1970) *Effective Communication of Ideas.* Van Nostrand Reinhold.

Wilcox, S W (1980) Communication courses for engineering students. *Engineering Education,* April.

Wise, A and Wise, N (1971) *Talking for Management.* Pitman.

Index